MAKING THE CASE

MAKING THE CASE

How to Be **Your Own** Best Advocate

KIMBERLY GUILFOYLE

HARPER

An Imprint of HarperCollins*Publishers*

HarperCollins books may be purchased for educational, business, or sales promotional use. For information, please e-mail the Special Markets Department at SPsales@harpercollins.com.

FIRST EDITION

Designed by William Ruoto

Library of Congress Cataloging-in-Publication Data has been applied for.

ISBN: 978-0-06-234397-0

15 16 17 18 19   OV/RRD   10 9 8 7 6 5

To three generations of Guilfoyle men,
Anthony Christopher Guilfoyle, Anthony John Guilfoyle, and Ronan
Anthony Villency

And to my mom,
Mercedes Gerena Guilfoyle,
who made it all possible.

"Success is not final, failure is not fatal: it is the courage to continue that counts."

—Winston S. Churchill

CONTENTS

PART II: ADVOCATING AT HOME

Those of you who watch me on television know me as Kimberly Guilfoyle. My producer and colleagues also affectionately call me KG. But back in the days when I was deputy district attorney in Los Angeles, and before I became an ADA in the San Francisco district attorney's office, I was known as The Hurricane. The nickname was a nod to Rubin "Hurricane" Carter, the boxer who literally knew how to fight for his rights in and out of the ring. Carter had been wrongly accused of a crime, imprisoned for nearly twenty years, and ultimately freed after appealing his case several times. He then went on to become an advocate for other wrongly accused prisoners, proving his mettle in the process.

When you are trying someone for a crime, as I did in my early career, the consequences for the victim, the defendant, and their families can be grave. In many cases someone's life hangs in the balance, so you better be precise with your investigation, your evidence, your words, and your intentions. I strived to do that every day and still do. Defendants would groan whenever they saw me enter a courtroom because I had a reputation for coming armed with the facts and for winning cases.

Later, when I served as first lady of San Francisco, having been married to the former mayor of that city and current lieutenant governor of California, Gavin Newsom, my role was to champion the rights of *all* the city's citizens.

In time I moved into cable and broadcast journalism to report on and analyze high profile legal cases as host of *Both Sides* on Court TV and *The Lineup* on the Fox News Channel. My longtime fans will remember me too for my regular appearances on CNN and *Good Morning America*. I covered the Scott Peterson, JonBenet Ramsey, Natalee Holloway, Kobe Bryant, and Michael Jackson trials, among many others. Viewers told me that they appreciated the way I'd home in quickly on what makes a sound point and what makes a flawed one. And just as important, they appreciated my ability to explain the difference.

Currently, I am a host on two of Fox News Channel's popular opinion programs, *The Five* and *Outnumbered*, a legal analyst on *The O'Reilly Factor,* and a political/legal analyst on *Hannity*. All of this is how I came to be known as an *expert in making the case.*

Now when people stop me on the street they tell me how much I've influenced their thinking on today's most hotly debated issues. It's wonderful to hear their feedback. I really value what they have to say and am thrilled that they consider me an inspiration. More often than not, they ask me questions too. What they most want to know is how I do what I do.

These inquisitive people—especially the young ones who are searching for their place in the world—invariably ask where I studied. They not only wonder how I got such exciting jobs, but also they're eager to find out how I was trained. Many more want to know where my passion comes from and why and when I first became so outspoken in the interest of others. Some are just curious, but most are looking for ways to learn how to do the same thing themselves—not necessarily in a court of law or in the media, but in their daily lives. They want to learn how to effectively communicate their ideas, thoughts, needs, and goals in their own homes, schools, and workplaces, as well as in their larger communities. And in these increasingly divisive times, they want to do so in a manner that furthers constructive dialogue and action.

These people are my motivation for writing this book. I truly believe that anyone can learn to do what I do and apply it in *all* aspects of their life. Even you. *Especially you.* You picked up this book with the intention of finding out those answers, right? So rally caps on for you!

It's a universal truth that all people want to be heard and understood. Effective communication is what drives our individual and collective success. As always, I'm happy to share with you what I know about the skills and mental preparedness required to build, state, and sustain your position on any topic of relevance and importance to you so that *now you too can become an expert in making the case.*

I tell anyone who asks that I had an excellent education because I believe that's an important part of the equation. I graduated magna cum laude from University of California, Davis; studied law at Trinity College in Dublin, Ireland; and earned my juris doctorate degree at University of San Francisco School of Law. During that time—and certainly since then—I've had many amazing and insightful teachers, professors, and mentors. *But I also tell people that the greatest classroom is life itself. It holds every lesson ever to be learned.* You see, the very first appeal I made in the interest of another person occurred years before I held any of my degrees or titles.

When I was just eleven years old, my mother, Mercedes Gerena Guilfoyle, lost her long and painful battle with leukemia. As you might expect, her death was the defining moment in my life. Throughout her illness, I remember *making my case* with God as to why he should help this graceful, nurturing, passionate, artistic woman live a longer and full life. I had prayed before, but this case was by far my most important one. I tried not to make it about myself because I shared my mother with so many other people who relied on and adored her too. I thought God should hear that part of the argument. She was a loving wife to my dad and a doting mom to my brother as well as to me. She filled our home with music, dance, crafts, fantastic meals, and the most festive holiday and birthday celebrations. But she was also an extraordinary teacher who connected with her words and heart to the special needs students she taught, many of whom had complicated emotional and learning differences. She was beloved by these children and their families. And she was valued and respected by her peers, who knew what kind of patience, caring, warmth, intelligence, creativity, and commitment was required of her in a job that was especially difficult.

My appeal to God was very simple. As soon as my dad came home each night, I'd run downstairs to meet him. My first question would be "How is Mommy doing?" I gauged her progress on a scale from one to ten and would always pray for her to be at least the same as the day before or better. Often those prayers were answered. In the end though, God had different plans for my mother's spirit. In retrospect, I believe he did answer my prayers for her to live on, because in so many ways her presence is felt in my life to this day. Her strength and wisdom helped to shape me. It left an indelible mark on my soul. She gave me my kind heart. But her passing was still such a tremendous loss for us all. This person who filled my cup with so much was gone and I had to figure out what to do next.

As often happens, we learn our most valuable lessons in the toughest of times and that, in fact, happened to me. What I have discovered since losing my mother is that you can always advocate for the best health care possible, but death is not something you can negotiate. *A case, however, can be made for virtually EVERY-THING else in life.* That is my motto and it was certainly the firm belief of my incredibly wise, determined, and resilient dad, Anthony "Tony" Guilfoyle. Before I share the tools to help you live by that motto too, let me just tell you a little about how those vital skills came to me.

After my mom died it was expected that I would step up and take on some additional responsibilities at home, particularly with regard to the care and upbringing of my brother, Anthony, who was eight at the time. I prepared his meals, got him ready for school in the morning, helped him with his homework in the afternoon if he needed me to, and was generally there to support and watch over him. Fortunately, my dad never expected more of me than I was capable of giving, and we both knew that. I was a very precocious child who was classified as a mentally gifted minor. I spent part of my day studying with students two grades ahead of me. I was the type of child who never missed a day of school, who worked to get the best grades I could in every subject, and who stayed up to all hours of the night reading for pleasure. I am a classic type A personality. If anything, my father had to encourage me to slow down and enjoy life more, to not become too intense. He saw that I had a lot of the same gifts as my mother and his bigger concern was that I learn to channel my energies and showcase my talents so I could get everything from life that I needed in order to flourish.

My dad often thought that in her short time on this earth, my mother held herself back, and he didn't want that to be my experience too. There were so many things about her that only he knew. He wished more people could have seen what a great singer, dancer, poet, and artist she was, but my mother was shy about her accomplishments. Don't get me wrong—she was a very determined and strong woman. When she came here from Puerto Rico she learned English and quickly assimilated into the American way of life. But my father recognized that she, like so many other women, tended to be modest and put others' needs before her own. It would be easy for me to do the same, especially since I was charged with looking after my brother. So his life mission was to teach me, and of course my brother, how to advocate for ourselves. Our whole family understood—especially in light of my mother's death—that life is short, so it was important to know how to make your case, and how to make it count. My father didn't want us to downplay our talents or to think there would always be another opportunity to put ourselves out there because you never know—maybe this is your time, your moment in the light. He also never wanted us to live with the regret that we didn't go after something we thought we should have pursued. He wanted us to be confident. To that end, he taught us to always do our best, to admit if we made a mistake, and to try again to make things work out better. Once we became our own best spokespeople, he made it clear that we were to use those same skills to help advance the causes of those who had not yet found their own voices. He taught us to think of others—even strangers—with the same compassion we feel for our loved ones and ourselves.

This wasn't just his philosophy; it was his day-to-day practice. There are so many wonderful examples in my childhood of how he worked these lessons into our daily lives. I remember, for instance, his reaction when my best friend Maura Devlin was running for president at our all-girls private school, Mercy High, and I decided to be her campaign manager. I threw myself headlong into the effort as I do everything. I was determined to get her elected. I made posters and banners, and was very organized about getting out the vote for her. When I told my dad all about it, he said, "That's fantastic. I'm very proud that you're getting involved, that you love your school, and that you're supporting a good friend. She's a terrific candidate. With you on her side, I'm sure she's going to win." Then he said, "You know, Kimberly, you're smart, you're passionate, you care about people. Have *you* ever thought about running for office? It would be amazing if you did something like this too." So I ran for vice president and Maura and I became a real dynamic duo. My dad was right. He wasn't encouraging me to run for the same position as Maura. I would have felt uncomfortable about that, but he was encouraging me to throw my hat into the ring in some significant way so I could share my ideas and do more to make the school an even better place for my classmates and myself. He believed there is great nobility in working to help others. He was also convinced that we grow and learn immeasurably from these kinds of efforts. Being vice president allowed me to do just that. I was happy my dad inspired me to make that leap.

My father encouraged me to do the same when it came to sports. During my sophomore year, I told him I wanted to try out for cheerleading and that two of my best friends, Maura Devlin and Sharon Thompson, were on the squad. Once again, he said, "That's fantastic. You've got great school spirit. You'll do an amazing job. But I've got to tell you, you've been blessed with tremendous athletic ability. Why don't you try out for a team instead? I support you either way, but how about getting in there and actually helping them win, not just cheering them on?" So I did. I tried out for the softball team and I made it. I was captain that year and co-captain in subsequent years. I had such a great time. It was fast pitch—a game I was happy to discover I really excelled in. We went on to win the championship that season and every season thereafter. I loved it so much, I thought about playing in college, but I was swayed by the impracticality of juggling practice, games, and all my prelaw studies. Nevertheless, I carry a certain team spirit with me in all that I do and am a big baseball fan to this day. *Go San Francisco Giants!*

Sports actually figured into my dad's philosophy about advocating for yourself in a big way. He really believed that physical strength and mental strength went hand in hand. So after my mother's death, he sent my brother and me to Ralph Castro's school for shaolin kenpo karate. Great Grandmaster Ralph Castro has trained and developed top black belts for more than fifty-five years. Shaolin kenpo is designed to teach its students sports competition, self-defense, and an offensive fighting system that involves both mind and body. One reason we chose this discipline and school is because shaolin kenpo goes beyond mastering specific martial arts movements. Developing mental discipline, respect, and high moral character were important aspects of our training.

My brother even won his division in the California Karate Championships. I told him that was thanks to all the training fights and butt whoopings I gave him when we practiced in the backyard. I regularly trained and sparred against men at this school. This made me tough and confident. I can handle myself. In college, I studied tae kwon do. In addition, my dad introduced us to boxing and kickboxing. He used to have us work out with a heavy bag in our basement. He bolted it securely to the ceiling, so imagine our surprise when one night, after a vigorous round of boxing and spinning back kicks, I knocked it right out of its mount. This big Everlast heavyweight bag just fell down. I thought, "Oh my God, I'm going to get into so much trouble," but my dad just came down the stairs, saw what happened, and said, "Oh yeah. That's my girl." He loved it. I knocked it right out of the ceiling. My father always used to tell me that whatever a guy could do I could do better. He was determined to raise my brother and me to be strong warriors. I was a sensitive and kind child and a little bit shy, but I became a mentally strong person through my father's coaching and my physical pursuits. I still love to box with my trainer, Harvey, who also officiates a lot of HBO professional fights.

There were lots of other ways that my dad taught me to be my own best advocate. I can't tell you how many times he sent me to my room to build my case. While I was growing up, he would say, "Don't ever be afraid to ask for anything, *BUT BE PREPARED.* Think about why you want it and why I should say yes. Have your best supporting reasons ready at the quick." So I took him up on the offer many times. When I was vice president of the senior class, I had to organize a class trip to Mazatlán, Mexico, that required us to stay overnight in a hotel for several days. I remember standing on the landing before the stairway that led up to the third floor of our home where the master bedroom was. I slowly climbed the steps. I was so nervous to ask his permission to go, but I had my notes clearly in my mind. I entered his room. He was sitting at his desk. He saw that I was a little tense, so he repeated his mantra, "Okay, go ahead. I may say yes, I may say no, but you always ask me. Right? Don't ever be afraid to ask." (You can see now why I'm always willing to entertain other people's questions!) So I gathered my composure and said, "Dad, I'd like to be able to go on the class trip and these are my reasons why: This trip has happened every year for many years. It's well supervised. We'll have a lot of adults with us. Here's the itinerary listing the specific events we've planned and their locations. This is where we're staying and all the necessary contact information. The hotel and the sites we are visiting are all in safe areas. There were no casualties, incidents, or problems in prior years when other groups of girls went. This is a structured event being sponsored by an all-girls Catholic school. The school understands its obligation to keep us safe as well." (*He told me to be prepared!*) Then I provided him with a list of parents who had given their children permission to travel. I made sure the list contained the names of people he knew well enough to call so he could talk over the pros and cons with them. I also told him that there were some parents who would only sign their daughters up for the trip if I was attending and could serve as their guardian since they were not yet of age and I was turning eighteen before the trip took place. I said, "Dad, these parents believe in me because of their own interactions with me and because of their daughters' relationships with me. They trust me to be the one responsible for them in another country. I think that says a lot about me, and how I am known to exercise good judgment. I planned this trip and I take it seriously as an event that can bond the class and as an experience that can also help prepare me for being away from home before I go to college."

You must understand that letting me go was a huge step for my dad. When my mother was dying, he promised her many times that he would look after me and make sure that I didn't fall in with the wrong people or falter in any way. He carried that heavy burden with him all the time. And even more amazing, he carried it alone. As an immigrant, he didn't have extended family nearby to help him out the way some other widowers might have had. It was clear in every decision he made that he wanted to be as incredible a parent to my brother and me as he knew my mother had always been. Those were big shoes to fill, but he wore them so well that I would call him every year on that special day in May to say "Happy Mother's Day" in addition to celebrating Father's Day with him the very next month.

Thankfully, my dad couldn't find fault with my presentation. After all, he had been the one to train me in the art of logical persuasion. I went to Mazatlán and it was everything I had hoped the trip would be and more.

Early on, my dad saw in me the potential to be a good advocate for myself and for my brother. He trusted in my values, morals, drive, and communication skills. He knew that ultimately the best way I could help my family and other people was to learn the craft myself. That's how I acquired the ability to think on my feet. The rest progressed naturally from there. The trip to Mexico was a sign for him that I was ready to do this on a larger scale—for others and in a more public arena. I had proven that I was ready to stand up and speak out for myself as well as for a noble cause when one presented itself. It was a big aha moment for me too. *I had truly seen how the power of words and clear reasoning could help me accomplish my goals.*

Let me tell you a little something about this very smart man. When I think about all the great influences in my life (many of whom I'll talk about throughout this book), the person I credit the most with helping me be *me* is my dad—hands down. He was born in Ennis, County Clare, Ireland, and came to the United States when he was just twenty-one. He settled in San Francisco, where he worked in the construction trade with his uncle Michael Lynch. My dad was a contractor, building people's homes at first, but he also worked on key aspects of the city's infrastructure, most notably helping to build the on-ramp for the Golden Gate Bridge. He also worked for the Pacific Gas and Electric Company for a time and was honored for his role in getting San Francisco rebuilt and running again after the city's devastating 1989 earthquake. Prior to my dad's passing he was presented with the key to the city, the highest honor bestowed by the city of San Francisco. In addition, the Mayor's Office and the Board of Supervisors declared November 27 Tony Guilfoyle Day. The Golden Gate Bridge Association also observed a moment of silence when he died, as did the California State Assembly led by Assemblywoman Fiona Ma, all in recognition of my father's numerous contributions. And that's not all. My dad also proudly served in the U.S. Army. He viewed living in America as a gift and often said that joining the military was just one small way he could say thank you and give something back to this great nation. He never took his citizenship for granted and he instilled that same patriotism in my brother and me.

Through his work, my dad made lots of friends in and out of city politics and ultimately became an integral member of my former husband's inner circle. He worked intently on Gavin's successful campaigns for a post on the Board of Supervisors and later for his mayoral election. I smile every time I think of my dad's nickname—he was affectionately known as "The Godfather" because of his own leadership abilities. He was the one to rally the troops whenever the going got tough. He kept the campaign workers happy and motivated. He was the team's emotional constant. He was such a great communicator. He also ran back channels and advised Gavin on field strategy. But probably his greatest strength was as a sharp judge of character. He'd often tell us who could be trusted. He was amazing at taking the measure of a person's integrity. A *San Francisco Chronicle* reporter once said, "He's the kind of man you call Sir because you want to, not because you're being polite." While I clearly shared this special man with all of San Francisco, he was always my personal consigliere in all matters of life. As you can see, he groomed me first to be my own best champion, and then he widened the playing field as he saw I was more and more capable, because a belief in helping others was always at the core of who he was. He not only talked the talk, he walked the walk. He was a great role model.

Why am I telling you all of this? Because it's a timely and important message. *Making and winning the case is not a matter of just speaking loudly. It's a matter of saying what you've got to say clearly and convincingly and with your actions as well as your words.*

As I said earlier, everyone wants to be heard and understood.

You can see it in the news—trouble bubbles up in people's personal lives, in business, and in all parts of the world's social order when they don't feel as if they have a voice. For your own sake and for the sake of everyone else, you should all master the skills needed to help communicate better, using every tool you've got.

In the classroom of life, I have enjoyed many blessings and endured many hardships. It's been a little like taking an AP survival course. But I've been strengthened by it all. The death of my mother is just one example of how resilience often comes from adversity. The lessons I learned from my father and from my many incredible experiences—good and bad—could fill a book. And now they have. These lessons have led to my current success on television and before that to an undefeated record in the court of law. So whether you are seeking to better express your needs or comprehend another's in your everyday relationships with a teacher, boss, coworker, friend, significant other, spouse, child, ex, parent, or co-parent, this book can help you. If you are a young adult applying to college or graduate school, a recent grad facing fierce competition in a tough job market, an innovator seeking venture capital for a great new business idea, a woman fighting for equal pay, a member of a minority group struggling to overcome racial stereotypes, a homeowner renegotiating your mortgage rate, a patient navigating the medical system, a parent trying to get your young child into the best school for him or her, or a citizen seeking political representation that reflects your values too, this book is for you.

No matter what stage of life you are graduating from or entering, learning how to build and state your case is something *every* person in the world should know how to do. And I just happen to be deeply passionate and experienced enough to guide you. In so many ways this is what I believe I was born to do. I find great comfort, strength, and honor in helping people find their voice. In making sure they don't miss out on life's many opportunities. In developing within them the means to express themselves in all their interactions. In helping them achieve a better quality of life. I enjoy teaching others how to identify what it is they want. I love it when they find a way to shape and state their case because of something I said. I really wish to help people engage in further dialogue and avoid the roadblocks that set too many of them off track. I want to end miscommunication and misunderstanding. Most of all, I want to pave a way for positive exchanges to happen between people. That's how individuals and societies evolve, grow, and thrive. So if you want these same things for yourself, read on.

Between the concrete steps I suggest you take, I share stories from my own life because sometimes we're able to gain inspiration and purpose by hearing what someone else has been through. Perhaps you can take a little bit of courage from my journey and apply it to your own circumstances. You may even find yourself thinking, "Okay, so she had some setbacks too, but look how she overcame them. When one door closed, a window definitely opened." Listening to another's stories can also illustrate that there isn't only one path, one direction, or even one job. Each channels us to the next stage of life.

I took the time to introduce you to my father because my hope is that throughout this book you will not only benefit from my experience, but you will also benefit from his. While he passed away in 2008, his wisdom still resonates with me and I think it will resonate with you. So as I share lots of tips and strategies about how you too can be an expert in making the case, be on the lookout not only for examples of what I and others I admire have done, but also for my dad's everyday teachings and practices. I truly believe that our combined adventures and wisdom will serve as a realistic and effective guide.

Here's to your future success in all realms of life!

PART I
ADVOCATING AT WORK

CHAPTER 1

How to Land the Best Job in the World (for You)

While the point of this book is to help you become your own best advocate, I must admit something that even you may not be aware of: *you are already a far better self-advocate than you realize.*

If, as a child or adolescent, you successfully negotiated with your parents for a later bedtime or curfew; a new computer; concert tickets; or a bold fashion choice, haircut, or body piercing they weren't too crazy about, then you know what I'm talking about. If, as an adult, you successfully negotiated with your spouse or loved one for a new home, car, or other high-ticket item that was a stretch; a vacation at a far more exotic or adventurous destination than either of you might be used to; or any other indulgence, then you also know a lot more about this business of advocacy than you are letting on.

Somewhere in the midst of those conversations, you knew exactly what to say to speak to the other person's most reasonable self, to prop open their mind, to get them to respect your wishes, or to reassure them that your judgment could be trusted. You also knew where to draw the line if they didn't seem likely to agree with you on the first or second try. You may have even gone back and thought of more convincing points to help strengthen your position. Advocacy or negotiation of any kind is just like that. As you will discover repeatedly throughout this book, it is about knowing yourself and, just as important, knowing the person you are appealing to.

For many people, however, the first time they doubt their own power to get what they want is when they must advocate for themselves with a stranger or when the stakes are so high their perception becomes skewed. That's why job interviews are notoriously difficult for the vast majority of folks, no matter what their age. When you advocate with family members they know your whole history. You know theirs. You know how far to push and under what circumstances there is wiggle room. In the worst job interview situations, there is no such knowledge. It's not even like the college admission process, where your meeting is at least preceded by a tour of the school (so you know something about them) and a quick read of an essay you wrote (so they know something about you).

During job interviews, you wonder if you sound boastful when telling a stranger about your best qualities—or conversely, you worry that you aren't selling yourself well enough. It's hard to be sure how others will receive you when they have no larger context.

That is why before you even apply for a job, it's important to create some kind of intimacy. I don't mean sleep with your interviewer. *I mean really get to know yourself.* Get introspective. Try to discern what you are looking for in life, in an employer, and in a particular job. Be honest with yourself about what your qualifications are. Determine what you still need to learn to do that job effectively. I also mean that you should get to know your potential employer. Acquaint yourself with what the company may be looking for in a new hire as best as you can. Investigate their standing in the industry. Learn more about the people you will likely be working for. What accomplishments are they most proud of? What were their most recent innovations? What are their latest initiatives? How can you help further their goals? How can they help further yours?

Some of this is instinctive, but some of it is learned behavior too. I'll never forget my first job interview. I literally made something from nothing (or almost nothing), and I did it half on instinct and half on the basis of my dad's teachings. I landed my very first paying gig with what most people would definitely call no prior experience. When I was in high school I saw an opportunity that seemed to have my name written all over it, even though I clearly didn't have the qualifications for it on paper. What I did have, however, was confidence, resourcefulness, and a love for the work— to say nothing of an obsession with salami! That's right, my very first summer job at a deli counter is what propelled me into the amazing career I have today. To say I love salami is a gross understatement. I always thought they called it cured meat because it seemed to cure all my problems, as it did in this instance too. On this momentous occasion, I parlayed my love of salami and my many years of experience making sandwiches for my brother and myself into a *management position*. I didn't just go in asking to serve the next customer; I made my case for why I should have the *top* spot and I supported that case well. *I knew myself. I knew where I wanted to go in life. I wanted to be the very best I could be in whatever I pursued.*

The job was at a brand-new grocery store near my home. For all intents and purposes it was an entrepreneurial job too because the deli operated as a start-up business within the larger grocery store. When I met with the owner, Mr. Kim, I told him how hard I worked at school and at home, raising my brother ever since my mom died. I explained how I not only maintained a straight-A average, but how I also shopped for groceries, prepared meals, and kept a clean and orderly home. I wanted him to know how responsible I was, especially for my age. (My youth, of course, would have been the obvious deterrent to hiring me.) I also offered to make a delicious sandwich for him to prove my worth in the taste department. I wowed him with my knowledge of all kinds of salami from Genoa to Sopressata, and of course I talked about my fondness for honey baked ham and roasted and smoked turkey too. I told him how badly I wanted the job, how much it meant to me, and how hard I would work for him. (Attitude really does count.) I also told him that the second he didn't like my service he could let me go. (Always a good closing argument for me.) *I knew my qualifications for the job and I left no doubt in his mind about what those qualifications were.*

I had done my research. I went to the deli counter at a competing grocery store and saw that they didn't even have a pricing board, let alone a listing of the different types of sandwiches they offered. I then went to three other delis and copied down their prices. I made a lovely sandwich board of my own to present to him, listing our specials and touting all their mouthwatering ingredients. There would be no doubt that our customers were getting homemade flavor in every bite. I also set my prices five cents lower than the competition's. Needless to say, I got the job and business was soon booming. All the construction workers in the area came in at lunchtime for a hearty meal. To encourage repeat business, I threw in a free cup of coffee for my regular customers, which was actually funny to me because my dad was Irish so I had grown up in a tea-drinking household. I had never made coffee in my life. In fact, on the day we opened the deli, I asked my first customer to help christen the new coffee machine by brewing a pot with me. After that one stealth course, I was ready to do it on my own. *I had determined what I still needed to know to do that job effectively and I set out to learn it.*

At the end of the summer I got a big cash bonus from Mr. Kim and an offer to stay on permanently. I had made a higher wage as a manager instead of earning just minimum wage, and I also got to take delicious deli meats home for my family. And that's not all—I got a tremendous amount of experience dealing with the various vendors who supplied us and with the people we served. How nice was that? Money, food, experience, *and* a title! Not bad for a beginner, right?

I did a lot of things correctly in that first job interview, but there was even more to discover. If I had known then what I know now, I might have owned and operated a franchise of delis before I ever went off to law school!

Since that time, I have been witness to some of the best advocates in the world. If you have ever watched a prosecuting attorney in action, you understand what I mean. They know themselves; their own strengths and weaknesses; their needs; and the needs of their clients, the defendants, and just about everyone else in the courtroom. That's how they manage to be as persuasive before twelve strangers in such a high-stakes situation as any of you are when arguing your point with a loved one. They can do this because they are masters at reading people, and they also know how to tell a story that conveys all the pertinent details—a story that compels and holds another's attention. The best of them:

- Are very clear about their objective.
- Prepare a brief story about their client that reflects their character.

- Have all the facts at their fingertips.
- Consider the perspective of the other side.
- Know everything there is to know about the judge's leanings, pet peeves, and past rulings and have drawn relevant conclusions about jury members from close observation as well.
- Have consulted with the more seasoned attorneys around them to be sure that their case is airtight.
- Never ask a question that they do not know the answer to

Before I show you how to apply what they know to your own high-stakes quests, let me first address the elephant in the room: while youth unemployment is down sharply from a record 27.3% in October 2009, ten months into the Obama presidency, it is still high by historic standards. As of the writing of this book, it is 18.8%. Add to that, skyrocketing college tuitions, and by default student debt, and you can see that young people are still facing challenges. The combination of this additional debt and a high unemployment rate is forcing many of them to take jobs below their education level just to survive. Some are abandoning the hunt for higher paying jobs and heading to bars, restaurants, and manual labor for a paycheck. Settling for a job below their education level adds downward pressure to youth wages as well. A waitress makes far less than a production assistant at Google or Apple. Others are seeking alternatives, stepping up, and creating their own work as entrepreneurs. But just because these people are their own bosses doesn't mean they've skirted the need to prove themselves. In fact, they have to try twice as hard since they're required to pitch their services to both funders *and* clients. Clearly, even with an improved unemployment rate the pressure is still on for recent grads to convince others of their value. *There's no doubt that having the skills to make a strong case for getting hired, with or without experience, remains incredibly important.*

The good news is that there are tried and true ways for everyone to make their best case and to prevail, even under the most challenging circumstances.

TRIALS AND TRIBULATIONS

Although the overall job market was healthier when I first graduated from law school than it is today, I remember facing similar challenges in my field and city as young people are facing in almost every field and city now. The odds were very much against me too. I was a woman pursuing work in a highly competitive, male-dominated profession. I'm Latina—a first-generation American. I had no family connections in a town where connections definitely open doors. I was raised by a single parent after my mother died, so my responsibilities at home could have easily prevented me from getting the grades required to succeed. The fact that I had to work several jobs to pay for school could have hampered me as well. But from the time I was very young I knew I wanted to be a lawyer and nothing was going to stand in my way. My mother used to do a lot of outreach work with disenfranchised and underrepresented groups in and around the Mission District, where I grew up, and she always took me along with her. We also volunteered at nearby Indian reservations. It was important to her, just as it was to my dad, to help people in need. Because I saw so many victims of violent crimes come from these communities, it became really important to me as well.

To prove I am right about the possibility of prevailing even under tough circumstances, I must tell you that despite these odds, I was hired to fill a coveted position with the San Francisco district attorney's office as a prosecutor soon after graduating from law school. For those of you who don't know the legal system—that is almost unheard of. Hundreds of people with a minimum of two years experience as a practicing litigator or trial lawyer apply for the position each year—and reapply in subsequent years when they don't get in on their first or second try. Hundreds more apply to serve in full-time volunteer attorney positions or clerkships. It was as if I hit the jackpot—as if I won the job lottery! But passion wasn't the only thing that got me where I wanted to be. Knowing how to advocate for myself according to the rules I have mentioned is what got me there. So don't let the statistics get you down. With help from this book and your natural talents and abilities, you have a real shot at getting what you want too.

PREPARING FOR SUCCESS

How exactly did I get that job? The secret of that caper was a lot of preplanning.

I knew that to compensate for not having many contacts, I had to start *making* those contacts and gaining more experience. The way to do that was to get on the inside and that meant doing the one thing I still think is incredibly effective to this day. I pursued an internship.

You see, when I was still a student at the University of San Francisco School of Law, the San Francisco district attorney's office had a reputation as one of the toughest places to land a job, especially without extensive experience trying and winning cases. From the outside, it appeared to be a very exclusive club because so many of the attorneys and judges had gone to the same schools. Given the relatively low number of positions and how many of them would be filled by people in the know, I was sure I'd have to be superproactive if I was going to acquire the necessary experience to become a prosecutor for the city. Fortunately, I read about a mentoring program through my school that enabled students to do trial advocacy work. That's where select students are immersed in mock trials to help them learn all kinds of strategies from leading jurists and lawyers in the field. It was one of those rare opportunities to learn from the experts—to practice direct and cross-examinations, interview and prepare witnesses, and select juries. I immediately enrolled, thinking that while it would hardly give me all the experience I needed, it was a solid first step.

I hoped that when I completed this advocacy work I would be an attractive candidate for an internship I wanted that was also being offered through my law school. This internship focused specifically on narcotics prosecution. There were a limited number of slots, as usual, so I knew the competition would be fierce, but I was adamant about getting into that office because I was convinced it would help give me an edge over other applicants when I graduated and was looking for a more permanent job. My plan was to get sponsored by a practicing attorney. I had already gotten into the habit of going to court to watch various prosecutors in action, so I had a good idea of the person I wanted to ask. I had been following the career of an incredibly dynamic assistant district attorney named Michael Hartmann. He was exemplary in every way. He was full of passion and always used such different tools to help build and sustain his cases. You couldn't help but learn by observing him. He was very theatrical—the delivery of his closing arguments was always so effective. I really believe watching him in those early days helped shape me to be the DA I ultimately became. However, the more I thought about asking him to sponsor my entry into the prosecution internship, the more I realized I wanted to work as *his* intern instead. Of course this was no small favor. He'd have to create an internship position for me. And that's not all . . . every lawyer with active Bar status is given a Bar number so when they agree to sponsor someone, they are effectively lending their Bar number to that person. If you mess up a felony case under someone else's Bar number there are dire consequences for you *and* for the sponsor. Believe me, you don't ever want to negatively impact your own or someone else's Bar status. But Michael had so much skill and panache, I was convinced that if I was able to work with him—if I could just follow him around and breathe the same air he did—I would learn enough to rise to the occasion. I am thankful that Michael agreed to my request. I proceeded to learn way more from him than I could have in any classroom situation. To prove that I am not exaggerating about how much of a force of nature this man is, you should know that he went on to work in post-conflict states and war-torn Afghanistan, serving, among other roles, in peacekeeping missions as the first UN Prosecutor for Kosovo, as Senior Crown Prosecutor in High Court in the Solomon Islands, and as the senior adviser and manager for capacity building in justice and law reform in several post-conflict countries. He is currently the Chief of the Rule of Law Unit at the United Nations Assistance Mission to Afghanistan. Previously, he was the Transitional Justice prosecution advisor for AusAID's Regional Assistance Mission to Solomon Islands to the Office of the Director of Public Prosecutions; Chief, Justice Section, United Nations Mission in South Sudan; advisor to the Attorney General's Office of Indonesia for USAID's Change for Justice Project; Manager, Criminal Justice Programme, United

Nations Office on Drugs and Crime (UNODC) in Afghanistan; U.S. State Department/International Narcotics & Law Enforcement/JSSP advisor to the Attorney General of Afghanistan; International Prosecutor at the Supreme Court and District Courts for the United Nations Interim Administration Mission in Kosovo; Senior Fellow, Jennings Randolf Program for International Peace, United States Institute of Peace; Regional Team Leader, Judicial System Assessment Programme, United Nations Mission in Bosnia and Herzegovina; UNODC Country Representative, Anti-Corruption Project, Bosnia; and Senior Fulbright Scholar, University of the Punjab, Lahore, Pakistan. He was also adjunct faculty at the University of California at Berkeley School of Law (Boalt Hall), UC Hastings Law and USF Law. It doesn't get much more serious than that! This is the man who trained me to fight for justice.

Under Michael's guidance I was able to work on violent crime cases as well, so I fared far better working with him than I would have had I taken the internship I initially considered.

I can still remember my first case during that time as if it took place yesterday. It was a robbery case and the defendant didn't take the plea bargain. It was up to me to make the opening statements, to question the witness, the whole deal. *I was trying a felony case and I was still in law school.* Most people don't even get to try misdemeanors until after they pass the Bar. What got me through the jitters of that trial was knowing that I had prepared thoroughly enough to meet the standards of my mentor and that he believed in me enough to let me take the reins. I had garnered more experience and a greater sense of self-assurance from that experience than you can possibly imagine. Long after my internship ended I continued to watch and learn from the best and brightest around me. I gleaned so much from being in the company of other spirited and powerful DAs in my career, including the great

Paul Cummins, Phil Kearney, and Bill Fazio. *Putting yourself in a position to observe and work with the pros, whether you are paid or not, is key to helping you make the kinds of strides that set you out in front of the pack.* But as with anything, you really need to make the most of that privilege.

An internship is both a gift and a barter arrangement. Once someone shares their knowledge with you, it is only right that you use that knowledge to help them handle the workload they are putting off to teach you. Naysayers think it's never a fair exchange, and I agree with them, but *not* for the same reasons. They believe that internships reek of exploitation. They view it as a means for employers to get you to work for little or no pay in hard economic times. But in my view, *interns* almost always win, especially if they assert themselves from the start, are superclear about what they hope to achieve, and work really hard to get as much out of the experience as they give. In other words, when you make an internship the reciprocal relationship it is intended to be, the value of what you gain in exchange for your labor is incalculable. Remember, mentors can take years— often in high-risk situations—to learn what they know, while mentees get to jumpstart their careers in just months, cribbing from those same lessons. So try to level things by making an extra effort. Work off the value of the gift in the quality and quantity of work you do. And on those occasions when you feel underutilized, practice what you're learning in this book and speak up on your own behalf. Come armed with suggestions of responsibilities you truly are ready to handle.

There is one more merit to internships that should be considered before moving on: these positions are not only meant to provide you with an opportunity to prove to prospective employers how well suited you are to the field and that particular company; they are also intended to help you see if the field or company is well suited to you. It is all too easy to lose objectivity once you begin formally working for an organization and you get on that treadmill, busily meeting the goals it sets for you, and, I hope, meeting the goals you set for yourself. You can grow very comfortable very fast, even in the wrong job, because having an income and perks—however modest they may be compared with what you aspire to earn—can mask the fact that you are headed in the wrong direction. *Internships really do allow you to try a profession, company, and/or position out for size.* They invite you to consider a particular line of work as one of several options down the road. If you do your best for the duration of the internship, you will have enough experience to help you evaluate your long-term happiness in that field.

By the way, if you are not certain when an employer has to pay their interns and when they are exempt from doing so, note that under the Fair Labor Standards Act, the Supreme Court outlines six requirements that must be met for an exemption to be granted:

- The internship, even though it includes actual operation of the facilities of the employer, is similar to training, which would be given in an educational environment.
- The internship experience is for the benefit of the intern.
- The intern does not displace regular employees, but works under close supervision of existing staff.
- The employer that provides the training derives no immediate advantage from the activities of the intern, and on occasion, its operations may actually be impeded.
- The intern is not necessarily entitled to a job at the conclusion of the internship.

- The employer and the intern understand that the intern is not entitled to wages for the time spent in the internship.

These stipulations ensure that in an unpaid situation the intern is deriving greater value from the relationship than the employer. As always, being educated about your rights and the measures already in place to help protect you from being exploited is yet another way to advocate for yourself.

If you approach internships with all of that in mind, they can truly be a win-win for everyone. If you are still not convinced that an internship is the way to go, consider what happened to me next.

When I finally graduated and applied for that prosecutor job I had been dreaming about all along, I was extremely well prepared. I had convinced someone of Michael Hartmann's stature to trust me with his own Bar number, cases, and license to practice law—and I had worked off that debt, while also gaining enough evidence to show my future employers what I could do for them. I also confirmed for myself that this was the right profession for me. It wasn't easy, but I landed my dream job through diligence and strategy even though it didn't seem at all attainable at first.

But enough about me—did you know that many other public figures got their start this way too? For instance, my friend and colleague Anderson Cooper interned for the CIA during his college years before becoming the exceptional investigative journalist he is today. As he has said, "I was nineteen years old, and like many college students was curious about a variety of careers." Internships are great for exactly that reason. With just a short-term commitment you get to explore an option you might not have otherwise tried.

And perhaps the most famous example is that of Steve Jobs,

who at just twelve years of age cold-called Bill Hewlett to ask for some spare parts to use in a frequency counter he was building for a school project. It seemed like the most natural thing in the world for him to do. Jobs has said, "I never found anybody that didn't want to help me if I asked them for help." As a result of his initiative, he landed an internship that same summer at Hewlett-Packard. A dream, and ultimately a legacy, grew from his initiative. Can you imagine if he hadn't placed that call? He took a chance and today his dream, Apple, is even more successful than ever before. The company's first quarter performance in fiscal 2015 was amazing. It posted record quarterly revenue of $74.6 billion and record quarterly net profit of $18 billion, fueled largely by all-time high iPhone, Mac, and App Store sales. How cool is that?

There are countless other people whose careers were launched this way, from Oprah Winfrey to Bill Gates. And most pay the blessing forward by employing interns in their businesses today. It is possible for you to do the same in your field of interest with a comparable investment of energies and a solid game plan. Who knows what could be in store for you after your promising intern experience.

SECURING YOUR FIRST SALARIED POSITION

If garnering some practical, albeit unpaid, experience is step one, then step two is going through some intensive training to present that experience in the best way possible during your first official job interview. I like to call this phase *Make the Case Boot Camp*.

It's worked wonders for me every time. What makes completing these exercises tough at first is the degree of honesty you'll need to assert with yourself and the degree of effort you'll need to apply to be as effective as you can be. I promise you though, if you develop these muscles, you will find your strength. Flex these muscles and you *can* win your case.

It is always necessary to be clear with yourself about what you're pursuing. Most people believe when they are interviewing for a job that the objective is to *get the job*. They assume they'll figure out how to do it once they are hired. However, to land the right position you need to look past the point of entry. You need to think about what you will be doing in that role day-to-day. When you have a clear idea of what your prospective employer will want from you, what you can deliver to meet those demands, *and* what you can possibly learn along the way to improve yourself, you can accurately pitch your skills *and* show genuine enthusiasm for the experience of working there. When it is evident that both parties have the potential to gain something of real value, it is a job most definitely worth making the case for.

You should also develop a one-minute spoken memoir. This is the succinct story you'll share about yourself during your interview. It should sum up who you are and how you wish to be viewed by your future employer and peers. For example, "I am Kimberly Guilfoyle. I've wanted to be a prosecutor for as long as I can remember. After my mother died when I was eleven years old, my father taught me to advocate for my brother and myself. I set my GPS for this job at that time and every stop along the way has helped me gather the experience necessary to get here. All the skills I learned as a kid volunteering with my mother to help Native Americans and people in need in the Mission District, and throughout my internships at law school, have prepared me to advocate on behalf of victims and their families and to be a fair, just, and hardworking representative of the San Francisco district attorney's office."

After you've drafted your spoken memoir, spend some time looking within for the evidence and confidence needed to support your story. In other words, dig deep to find all the reasons why you are the right person for the job. Reflecting on all of your experience—your early achievements as well as the most recent ones—will remind you of specific skills you've developed and exercised that you may have forgotten about. Keep the accomplishments that best apply to the job you are pursuing fresh in your mind, so you can use them as examples. Then pocket the rest to give you added comfort and security. *Once you have assured yourself of your qualifications, you will have both the poise and the facts to convince others.*

Another essential step is becoming one with the subject. Before your interview, try to anticipate all the questions you may be asked, even the less obvious ones, so you are as well versed on the subject matter as you can possibly be. Frame your answers in advance so you have clear and concise responses to draw upon. The more these answers are second nature to you, the more knowledgeable and in command you will appear and actually be.

Knowing the answer to any possible question also helps you control and drive the conversation to the selling points you want to make in the event the interviewer's line of questions hasn't given you a chance to do that earlier, and you still believe they are valuable points to note. I anticipated everything Mr. Kim might have asked me when interviewing for the deli management position. As a result, he knew he wouldn't have to question my judgment once I was on the job because I had proven that I'm the type to ask the necessary questions of myself even before events happen.

Also remember as you are becoming one with the subject to look for the loopholes in your logic or the places where you don't have the facts to support your reasoning. Be sure to fill in those gaps before your big meeting. If we've all learned one thing from Murphy's Law, it's that the subject you wished you knew more about will come up no matter how great the odds are against it. And even if it doesn't come up, your confidence may have already been dashed by the subconscious fear that it will.

Throughout this entire process, you should also be remembering the three Rs: research, research, research! You may believe you have all the facts necessary to prove you are right for the job because you can speak well about your own assets and experience. But don't make prepping for the interview *all* about yourself. Reading up on the latest trends in the industry, your potential new boss, and the company and how it stacks up against the competition will provide you with a broader perspective that will set you apart from all the other candidates. *In short, be better prepared than anyone else.*

To be sure you've covered all your bases, find a specialist, pro, authority, or the equivalent of a Mac Genius in your field to talk to. As you follow all of the advice above, you may find that you still need more insight than reading up on the subject can provide. That's when you should call in reinforcements. Don't be afraid to ask other people for help. Think about everyone you know—school alumni, friends of your parents, friends of friends, anyone who is already on the path you'd like to be on—and arrange to ask them questions about how they got where they are; what bumps in the road you can expect to encounter; how to avoid those bumps; and, of course, any other relevant job or life experience they have to offer. Prepare specific questions before your meeting with them so the conversation runs smoothly and you are respectful of their time. And always follow up with a thank you note. Throughout the years, I have kept the names and contact information of everyone of interest I have met. I keep in touch regularly, sending an email or text to congratulate them if I've heard good news about events in their life and career, and sometimes I write to just share good news about mine. Never be afraid to ask questions or to network. It is one of the most valuable tools available to you in all of life.

If you discover that the gaps in your knowledge are bigger than you thought or that they may prevent you from being qualified for the job you are interested in, accept the fact that your timing may not be right. All too many hiring managers say recent grads aren't ready for the jobs they're seeking and lack the solid work ethic that could possibly make up for their deficit in knowledge. If you feel unprepared after doing what is suggested, perhaps you should seek an apprenticeship or an internship so you can develop the skills you need to fill the role you are applying for more completely. If an internship doesn't exist, propose one or offer to fill the position on a trial basis or for reduced pay until you can do it fully. Remember how well my internship with Michael Hartmann served me? And remember how well the highly successful people mentioned earlier fared.

Lastly, I always recommend that you cross-examine yourself. What I mean by that is think hard about whether what you are going after is what you really want. Ask yourself if there are different opportunities out there within reach that might serve your purposes better. If not, commit and act decisively. *Please don't confuse this self-reflective step with wavering.* It's intended to help you continue to pursue your course comforted by the knowledge that you've looked at other options. If there are other opportunities you think might suit you better, devise a plan to pursue those too. In my case, cross-examination made me realize that securing an internship with Michael Hartmann would be better for me than getting the prosecution internship I thought I wanted. I had to weigh the pros and cons of being one applicant for a job that didn't exist versus being one *among hundreds* of applicants for a job that only a few would get in the end. In this instance, cross-examination led me on a different course than I originally planned, but at other times it confirmed that I was on the right track. In either event, it's an incredibly useful tool.

If, in the end, you feel comfortable with how much there is for you to discover, you are passionate about the position and field, and you have a history as a quick study in areas you are most interested in, trust that you will be able to educate yourself as you go along. Some people say "fake it till you make it," but I don't believe in faking anything. Be straight with yourself about what you still need to learn and commit instead to grow until you know. You can get past any gaps in your knowledge quickly if you make a mental note of the people around you who do their jobs well. Observe what they do and see if their practices can apply to your own situation. Don't be shy about asking them to share advice with you. They will very likely be flattered enough to meet and talk with you.

My dad would probably offer one additional piece of advice. He'd no doubt tell you to *make history.* That's not to say do something you will become famous for, although you very well might. What it means is gather as much experience as you can, wherever you can. The more you challenge yourself and test your limits, the more success you will enjoy, and the more history you will have to draw upon for your next stage in life.

He'd also tell you that if you want something badly enough, you should fight for the opportunity—even if other people tell you it doesn't exist. He'd regale you with stories about how my obsession with soccer when I was seven or eight years old led my mom to ask the coach of the second-grade team to see if I could try out. Unfortunately, it was an all-boys team, but that didn't stop her. She asked him to give me a chance to show what I could do, saying, "If she's good, she should play regardless of gender. If she's not, then she shouldn't." After she made her case, I had a chance to make mine on the field. I was asked to join the team that very day. Right there is an example of how I was raised. Just because something isn't already established doesn't mean you can't pursue it, accomplish it, and blaze a path for others while doing it. As it turned out, my making the team set the precedent for one of my best girlfriends, Karen Hirsch, who loved soccer as much as I did, to play for the team too.

Both my mom and my dad taught me that everyone should have an opportunity to show their ability—even if they have to create that opportunity for themselves. What you do with that chance is up to you. To get the position on the team you are obsessing about, or the role in that company you have your heart and mind set on, you've got to impress the powers that be. *Want it. Believe it. Earn it. Show it. Only then will you get it.*

Follow these simple guidelines and you will have the necessary tools to build a case the way the most effective prosecutors do.

- Your objective will be crystal clear to your prospective employer because it is to you.
- Your one-minute spoken memoir or story will provide your interviewers (aka your judge and jury) with greater perspective on your character.
- Your résumé and advanced preparation will ensure that the facts to make the most persuasive case are at your fingertips.
- Your ability to address any concerns your interviewers may have evidences your consideration of their perspective.
- Your knowledge of the inner and outer workings of

the industry and company indicate your access and ability to network and consult with experts in the field.

- And the questions you already know the answer to are the questions that will impress them and seal the deal.

Everything you need to build and present an airtight case for yourself is in your possession. You've even gotten an added dose of confidence from my dad. Now all you have to do is go for it.

MAKING A CASE WHEN YOU'RE REAPPLYING FOR YOUR CURRENT JOB

There is another phenomenon in today's job market that is requiring many to sharpen their case-building skills. Advances in technology and design, along with rapid shifts in consumer preferences, are causing people in some industries to periodically reapply for the positions they already hold so employers can be sure their employees are keeping pace with their evolving businesses. Because trends are so fleeting, even the youngest of you are experiencing this. If this is happening to you, I believe the following advice will not only help you make your case with integrity, grace, and resolve, but with success too.

To ensure your relevance, keep up with all the new developments in your field and in the general news. Read related blogs, set Google Alerts to topics relevant to your work, and check out what's trending online.

Remain positive. Change does not come easily for many

people. But if you look at change as a chance to acquire new skills and, in this case, as a chance to possibly redefine your current job so it is more rewarding for you and your employer in the long term, it really can end up being a great benefit to you. As it turns out, going after your own job again can also help you form the very habits you hope to develop by reading this book—it actually provides a formal opportunity for you to practice what you are learning about being: your own best advocate.

Always be willing to push yourself further. Try to embrace change whenever you encounter it. To keep it from being too intimidating, think about all the exciting possibilities you would miss if you didn't try. To help yourself remain open to new experiences, tell yourself, "This isn't going to be bigger than me. I'm going to jump right into it. I'm going to master it. I'm going to get on it and do it better than I ever expected to." In other words, never let your fear fill your head with lots of counterproductive and self-limiting thoughts. Challenge your inner optimist to get there first and fill your mind with motivational thoughts instead.

In the words of my dad, "Always be prepared." Keep an ongoing list of your accomplishments, especially as these accomplishments relate to new and emerging trends, tools, and practices. Be sure to add your most recent ones to the top, and to update it regularly so you are always ready to represent your most current strengths.

Also, be sure to plan ahead. Set goals for yourself that not only help you acquire new cutting-edge skills, but that also help your company make forward strides in a changing landscape. Conduct a private performance review with yourself every month, where you take a measure of how well you are fulfilling these goals. When you meet with your superiors for your interview, you'll be ready to prove that you are not only qualified to keep your job, you're qualified to change aspects of the position and the company's standing so they are just as relevant in the marketplace as you now are.

And last, but not least, be inclusive. As you draw your boss's attention to some of your new findings, offer to teach your peers about what you've learned. *Sometimes making the case for yourself means making the case for others.* Leadership is especially needed in times of change, so develop and exercise those skills too.

MAKING YOUR CASE WITH A NEW EMPLOYER AFTER BEING DOWNSIZED

What I didn't tell you yet about landing that coveted prosecutor job in the San Francisco DA's office is that some serious sea changes occurred within months of my arrival. Arlo Smith, who had served as the DA for sixteen years, hired me while he was running for reelection. After he was defeated by Terence Hallinan, Terence invoked what's known as the LIFO principle (last in, first out) upon the recommendation of one of his senior staff members. Essentially, he terminated the positions of the fourteen most recently hired people to make room for those who had helped him during his campaign. I was one of those fourteen people. I was crushed. I had worked so hard to get there and it was over all too fast. So many people told Terence after they heard the news that I was an incredibly strong asset who should have been kept on, but what had been done could not be undone. The government paperwork had already been processed.

The day I got that pink slip, I was supposed to turn my ID and badge in to Paul Cummins, the number two DA at the time and a giant among trial lawyers. (Paul has argued more than two hundred cases in his career, fifty of which were for murder.) I was so devastated at the thought of leaving this job that I loved so much that I asked him to hold my things for me. I was determined to return someday and that was my way of letting people know that was exactly what I planned to do. In a defiantly bold moment, I introduced myself to Terence in person, told him my story, and declared that I would get my job back. I wanted him to remember me. I wanted to make one last pitch. I wasn't ashamed, embarrassed, or deterred. I knew I might be rejected again, but some things in life matter that much. He was as nice under the circumstances as anyone could be. By the way, he was also apologetic over the loss of my position because by this time he had heard quite a bit about my abilities and work ethic from my peers and colleagues, as well as from judges. The layoffs happened shortly after the O. J. Simpson murder trial ended and just about the same time as the LA DA's office announced that it was expanding. Even though I would be up against the same class of lawyers who worked incredibly hard and amassed invaluable experience interning on that historical case, I took the leap and applied there. Armed with the same list I would have presented to Terence Hallinan, outlining all the reasons why I was the prosecutor to have on his team, I wowed the interviewers. In fact, I brought a book in with me and showed it to them. It was an old criminal law primer, but it had a very special meaning to me. I told them, "This book represents my dream, my legacy. It's why I want to be a prosecutor." My mother had originally given it to my older cousin Ike Ortiz, who was chief of police in Foster City, California, when he first entered the police academy. She always had a passion for criminal law too and even studied it for a while with the intent of pursuing a career in it. It was what drove her volunteer work in impoverished neighborhoods. But she sacrificed her opportunity to pursue this profession so she could raise children. I always wanted to carry the justice torch forward for her, especially as I shared a passion for the law too. When I first became an ADA my cousin passed the book along to me with a beautiful inscription telling me how proud my mother would have been of me for all of my accomplishments and for following my dreams. When I left San Francisco, the fire in me burned even brighter. I really wanted to carry that torch— that legacy— forward for her and for me. I proceeded to get 100 on both my written and oral tests. It was clear there was a hunger in me. I was wounded but not defeated. I learned that the best you can do is:

- Carry your head high.
- Remind yourself of your strengths.
- Look constructively at where you can improve.
- Set new goals for yourself.
- Be straightforward with prospective employers about what happened if need be, but don't dwell on the subject.
- Lay out your best case, bearing in mind all the tools I've shared in this book.

These rules apply to your first job interview as well as your umpteenth interview, and to external interviews as well as to internal ones.

The same goes for those of you who will be or have already been fired due to a direct conflict rather than due to a reorganization or reduction of staff. Shortly after Jill Abramson, the former executive editor of the *New York Times* was abruptly dismissed in May 2014 amid speculation that she and her publisher clashed over her tough management style and issues of compensation parity (both of which are hot topics for women in the workplace and which we'll address in detail later), she gave an inspiring commencement address at Wake Forest University, where she talked about what it means to be resilient. She reflected on wisdom her dad had shared with her and her sister years earlier. He was the type of man who encouraged both of his daughters to show what they are made of, especially when encountering trying circumstances. She said, "It meant more to our father to see us deal with a setback and try to bounce back than to watch how we handled our success." The overriding message of her speech was to always find a way to press on in the face of disappointment. Her words resonated with me. As I—and I'm sure many others—have discovered when facing challenges in our careers and in everyday life, success lies very much in how you pick yourself up after a fall.

Although I left the San Francisco DA's office in what was definitely a state of disappointment, I was still eager to show the world what I was made of. *I adopted the attitude that opportunity exists in uncertainty.* I returned to work there four years later, just as I swore I would, but not before getting some of the most amazing experience of my career in Los Angeles. I was better. I was brighter. I was stronger. I was a warrior. I became deputy DA in LA under the leadership of the formidable Gil Garcetti and was trained by Stephen Kay— the coprosecutor with Vincent Bugliosi in the case against Charles Manson for Manson's role in the infamous Tate-LaBianca murders. My experience there instantly took me to the next level in my career. Given the diversity and size of LA, I got to prosecute a wide range of cases back-to-back, dealing with everything from narcotics, domestic violence, kidnapping, robbery, and arson to sexual assault and homicide. Whereas I thought leaving my old job was the very worst thing that could have ever happened to me, it turned out to be one of the best. When I did finally return to the San Francisco DA's office, it wasn't to get my old job back; it was to get an even greater position as assistant district attorney. It was a very triumphant homecoming.

Should similar unexpected twists, drama, and plot turns occur in your career, be open to what lies ahead. And remember to be the change you want to see. *Sometimes making the case can mean turning the worst-case scenario into the best one.*

CHAPTER 2

Dressing for the Part

How many times have you woken up feeling a little nervous about a presentation you are making at work, the performance review you have scheduled, or the new boss you're meeting? You poke your head into the closet and just want to shout "*dresscue* me!" You look for something in there that will save you from the jitters you're feeling even though you've prepared in every other possible way. You know it's not the violet sweater that brings out the Liz Taylor in your eyes. That's the totally wrong vibe. Maybe it's that power suit with the pencil skirt that always makes you walk a bit taller. Or if you're a gentleman, it's that bespoke suit, tailored to fit you perfectly in every way. *All of this deliberation is the sound of your subconscious mind telling you that clothes can help advocate for you, especially on days when you need an extra dose of confidence.*

Clothes speak to us. They tell us they've got us covered—that they'll help us make the perfect first impression if we promise to do the rest. We depend on them to help us make a personal statement, and when we've taken the time to carefully cultivate the items in our wardrobe, they often do. They really are incredible tools of empowerment.

Why do we rely on clothes so much? And on our appearance in general? *It's because we all know—even if just subliminally—that other people's opinions of us are formed within seconds of our meeting them.* It's been proven that our accessories, hairstyle, and makeup indicate more about us than we can actually say in such a short span of time. We speak volumes about ourselves through all aspects of our appearance. If we are dressing with care and thought we are letting people know that we respect ourselves—and them—enough to make the extra effort. If used the right way, our attire can be one of our strongest assets.

When I was in high school I worked at a Clothestime store to help pay for my own wardrobe and to save money for college. I watched people fall in love with an article of clothing because they thought it truly reflected who they were. They would sometimes buy the item in multiple colors or come back for another just like it when the original purchase was worn out. I was no different. I had a favorite T-shirt I wore every day because it promoted one of my absolute guiding principles. Written across the chest was the word *plan*, and running down from the letter *a* was the word *ahead*. Of course, *plan ahead* was and still is my motto. I couldn't stop wearing that T-shirt. I'd race to get it out of the wash as soon as the laundry was done. I wish I could wear it right now. I was the type of person who was always thinking, "What's my next play? How am I moving the ball forward? How am I getting it into the goal?" That T-shirt said it all.

My point is that even when your clothes aren't that literal they can still speak on your behalf. They can attest to your legitimacy, power, or strength. They can support a case for how earnest, reliable, or creative you are. How prudent or daring. And they can do it all visually, so they are, I hope, reinforcing the same impression you're making with your choice of words and actions.

I think I intuitively understood how much appearance counts from the time I was very young. I went to an all-girls Catholic school when I was growing up where I had to adhere to a dress code. The dress code placed value on the integrity of our appearance rather than on style per se.

I realized how important that message was when I became a prosecutor and had to dress for court. I knew from that early training how to comport myself. Whenever I was trying a case, I would wear a nice, well-made, but understated suit. I'd tie my hair back in a French twist so it was off my face, and I wore little or no makeup and very minimal jewelry, if any. I never wore anything racy, low cut, or too short. I kept it simple and clean since I didn't want to alienate anyone or distract from my message. I was the guide, not the show. I wanted everyone present to know that I had respect for the justice system.

I selected jury members using those same indicators. I wanted to be sure they had respect for the process and that they understood the seriousness of what they were being asked to do. I wanted to know that they would responsibly evaluate the evidence, and be aware that their conclusions had an effect on someone else's life. That they would consider the victim and what happened to him as well as what would happen to the defendant, who was potentially going to be sent away to prison. I really disliked when people came to court in surfer shorts and flip-flops. I wasn't expecting them to wear a three-piece suit, but I did expect them to show respect for the process, the court, the judge, their fellow jurors, and themselves, as well as for the victim and the seriousness of the charges. I wanted them to show that they knew this wasn't some picnic or vacation. That the consequences were real.

How I dressed and how the jurors dressed communicated our level of seriousness about the process to each other. It was a powerful—if unspoken—dialogue we engaged in together. My appearance was always the first sign I gave them that I was a committed advocate for the victims and families I represented.

Those of you who are fans of *Law and Order* know that appearances matter for witnesses and defendants too. How many street criminals do you think own a suit before their hearing? Their lawyers know better than most people that clothes can be your best advocate when trying to make a good impression . . . or when trying to undo a *bad* one.

Let me tell you a real-life story about how a change of clothes helped a victim effectively advocate for herself in one of the more difficult cases I've tried in my career. It involved a young impoverished woman—a single mother—who was shot sixteen times at close range by her boyfriend when he suspected that she set him up in a drug rip-off. This boyfriend just happened to be a charismatic gang leader with the Venice Shoreline Crips. His name was Isaiah Eugene Caldwell, but he was also known by the street moniker C. Capone. He was the type of man who, despite being incredibly dangerous, exuded a certain kind of charm. You guessed it: he dressed impeccably and carried himself with tremendous confidence and swagger. Nothing about him on the surface fit the stereotype of a shot caller of a gang. He was a highly intelligent, well spoken, very sophisticated individual with a strong personal style. It didn't seem likely that the victim, Star Smith, would have nearly his presence or believability on the stand because she had just been released from the hospital and was still healing from the psychological and physical wounds inflicted on her in the attack. She was visibly diminished by the whole ordeal. She hardly had the money for new or court-appropriate clothes, but Star was going to be her own witness so it was important for me to help humanize her in the eyes of the jury—to make sure she had every opportunity for her story be heard, which included looking presentable. Sometimes it's hard for me to fathom that a jury can be more sympathetic to an offender than to a victim, but people come to situations with all kinds of preconceived notions and the difference in the victim's and defendant's appearances did not seem as if it was going to help our case much unless we corrected it.

On the night of the crime, Star simply thought she was going out on a date with Caldwell. Instead, he and his friends set out to kill her as payback for the burglary at his home. He believed she told some rival gang members about the money and narcotics he kept in his apartment. This attempted revenge murder was domestic violence at its worst. It nearly cost Star her life and the custody of her child. I've seen it many times before: poverty dehumanizes people, often victimizing them twice. But I firmly believe that truth speaks. Star had to make her case and I had to do everything I could to help her do that effectively. Because the defendant wasn't caught at the scene of the crime, it was going to come down to credibility. The jury would be weighing her word that he was one of the shooters against his word that he wasn't. There was going to be a showdown in the courtroom.

You can only imagine how daunting facing your assailant and testifying against him after such a vicious, heinous attack can be, especially if he is as powerful a man as Caldwell was. So much of advocating for victims is about trust. I had to convince Star to let me help her tell her story. It was imperative from the start that she have confidence in me. Thankfully the Los Angeles district attorney's office has an excellent victim witness assistance program. The detective assigned to the case also earned her trust. Together we kept her safe, checked in with her three or four times a day, and prepped her for the kinds of questions she would field when she testified. But in addition to all of that, we also provided her with the appropriate clothes and attended to her hair, nails, and makeup. You cannot imagine how much this kind of attention can restore someone's self-esteem. These details are important. You don't want anything to ever dilute or distract from the message or your story. *I wanted the jury to push past any assumptions they might have otherwise made about her because of her appearance.* I wanted nothing to get in the way of her exercising her own courage. It was important that we impress upon the jury that she was a young mother, like any other mother, struggling to ensure her child's and her own survival.

In an interesting twist, I was asked by the defense attorney to talk to the defendant to help convince him that he should take the plea bargain deal we were offering. You see, in the court system, every case has its worth—a number that will make the parties settle, preventing them from going to trial and costing the taxpayers even more money. I knew Caldwell's defense attorney well as we had previously opposed each other in several other very serious cases. He knew I was fair dealing and I knew he was as well. The defendant was initially looking at a fifteen-years-to-life sentence, but the DA's office was giving him the opportunity to accept a determinate sentence instead—somewhere between fifteen and twenty years with the possibility of getting out after serving a majority of that sentence with good behavior. Despite the fact that the deal could potentially help Caldwell avoid spending all the remaining years of his life in prison, Caldwell wasn't interested. It appeared to me that he was counting on his well-crafted image to help him beat the charge. He had people lined up to testify on his behalf as character witnesses, including respectable members of the local boys club. He probably thought he could make the jury believe that Star lied and that he, in fact, did not attempt to murder her. I'll never forget the day I was brought into lockup to speak directly with this dangerous man. I was not fooled by his outward appearance—I knew the kinds of things he had done. We talked about the deal. We talked about the fact that he had made many poor choices in his life. Then I told him in no uncertain terms that he was about to make another poor choice. I urged him to take the offer. I said, "Do something for yourself here. You've been given this chance. It's an opportunity for you to get out. I am telling you right now as I sit here with you that I'm going to convict you. Then you are looking at a possibility of up to life behind bars." We went back and forth that way for a while, but in the end he wanted to roll the dice and gamble—to play the odds. I'm sure he thought he could hang the case. He had cultivated a certain image and was confident in that. He had an excellent attorney. He may have even thought that Star wouldn't show up—that she'd be too afraid to come forward—and that the case would get a mistrial and fall apart as a result. But I was not going to let that happen. I'm happy to say that Star bravely testified, the jury heard the truth in her words, and justice was served.

I sometimes wonder if Caldwell regrets the decision he made the day we spoke, but whether he does or doesn't, the lesson we can all take from this case is that Star had many advocates that day. She had me, the rest of the team at the Los Angeles DA's office, and herself. *The truth and the kind of proper attire that allowed people to trust what she was saying were her advocates too.* As for Caldwell, he proved that while clothes can say a lot about you, you must be able to back up the image you are projecting to the world for the clothes to convincingly do their part.

MODEL BEHAVIOR

Long before I used appearance to help make my case in the courtroom, I learned a lot about the language of clothing—*what* to wear, *how* to wear it, and *when* to wear it in order to say something subtle or bold about myself—in one of the best training grounds possible.

As many of you know, I paid my way through college and law school as a model. I was in ads throughout a wide variety of newspapers, catalogues, retail stores, and more. And yes, I modeled Victoria's Secret lingerie too. The experience was also filled with other life lessons that reinforced some of the most important ones about self-advocating.

I was discovered by a beautiful woman named Claudette Ahlstrom. She and her equally beautiful daughter were shopping at a Clothestime store in Davis, California, where I worked as a manager at the time. (The same store I mentioned earlier.) We struck up a conversation. It turned out that they were both models and that her daughter wanted to be a lawyer, just as I did. She was putting her modeling money away to finance her education. Claudette asked if I was a model too. When I said no, she began to tell me all the ways modeling was helping her daughter reach her goals. She was convinced that modeling could do the same for me. She offered to introduce me to her agent, but I was reluctant at first. She was so persuasive, however, that I did stop to think about it some more. When I finally warmed to the idea, she set up a meeting with Michael DeMartini, who was head of the New Faces division at Grimme, the San Francisco–based agency that launched the careers of Suzanne Somers, Christy Turlington, Jack Scalia, and many others. Grimme was a hot agency closely allied with Ford Models, so I was sent out quite frequently. Once they saw my test shots I did a lot of beauty and body work.

Luckily for me, lingerie bookings paid double the usual rate. Of course, I had to be assured that I wouldn't be asked to do anything I was uncomfortable with. (There's that instinct to self-advocate again.) Grimme provided that comfort, and I'm happy to say that I never participated in a shoot I felt badly about or regretted. I remember being very shy about doing a honeymoon shot with a male model in a bridal magazine one time, so I presented my case and the magazine ultimately agreed to let me do it alone. I told them that I really thought it would be more romantic, and just as sensual, to see the bride anticipating the moment when she would see her groom than to actually see the two of them together. It was beautifully photographed and turned out to be exactly what the client wanted. When you are modeling you really need to make a case to the consumer. You have to evoke a memory, an emotion, a feeling that ultimately compels them to want this item and experience too.

I'm very grateful for my modeling experience. It taught me a lot about having presence and confidence and how to focus on being my best self in any situation rather than focusing on the competition. In one situation I was the last of three hundred girls to be seen, and although the client had already decided on a previous model, I was determined to use the opportunity to show them how I moved, how relaxed I was in front of the camera, and how well I took direction, in the hope that they would reconsider their decision or at least remember me for a future ad. I owned that last slot of the day and guess what? They hired me instead of the model they had originally planned on using!

It wasn't always that easy though. Some girls struggled with rejection. I fortunately didn't have that issue, but hearing people talk about me—analyzing my face and body as if I wasn't even in the room—definitely took some getting used to. Part of advocating for oneself is putting others' views of you in perspective. It is learning to take criticism when it is valid. It is understanding that you may not have been able to communicate your worth in a limited period of time and that you will have to work on that skill more for future tries. It is learning to do your best in every circumstance. It is also understanding that some of the decisions that have an impact on your life are subjective. They may not always be a rejection of you so much as they are an embrace of someone else who is simply different—not necessarily better—than you. Advocating for yourself can mean many different things in many different situations. It can mean having high expectations for yourself, and it can mean trying harder when you don't succeed, but it never means beating up on yourself when you are disappointed. In fact, that is the opposite of advocating for yourself.

Modeling was also great because I got to practice asserting boundaries. I was vocal about what would be crossing a line for me, so I was never sent out on jobs that were out of my comfort zone. Many of today's models are so young they may not have experience knowing or communicating those personal rules to people who can influence their long-term careers. Fortunately, I was college-aged by the time I modeled and I also had prior work experience. That maturity helped a lot. I also knew modeling wasn't my endgame, so I didn't fear that saying no to some projects would pose problems for me at a later date. A sense of autonomy is important to maintain—even in your desired field—if you are going to be able to effectively self-advocate. You cannot fear the risk of losing your standing when you are trying to uphold your principles.

As with all my jobs, I also learned I could be self-sufficient while I was modeling. It was good to know that I didn't have to go to my dad and ask for money when he was already working so hard to provide for my brother and me in other ways. Asking him for money was always a hard thing for me to do. He would give it to me, of course, but I preferred to step up and earn it myself. To advocate successfully, you need to learn to stand on your own two feet. I know working several jobs at once sounds like the opposite of advocating for oneself. Sacrifice seems like an odd prerequisite for practicing something designed to get you everything you need. But modeling was very lucrative work and the income I made from that and my two other jobs helped me actualize my long-term aspiration of becoming a prosecutor, so I would definitely call that advocating for myself.

I knew it was time to end my modeling career, however, when I did an ad for a Teledyne showerhead that appeared in an especially widely read issue of *Sports Illustrated* magazine. The issue was focused on the World Series, and some of my colleagues in the San Francisco DA's office wondered aloud if the legs in the ad were mine. I knew right then and there that modeling had taken me as far as it could and that I would have to go forward without its further support. I had achieved my dream. I was in the district attorney's office and I will always appreciate that modeling helped get me there. But it was important at this crucial juncture in my career that I put forth one image and one image only. I needed everyone to know that my highest priority was being a DA. When I left the modeling business, I graciously thanked my agents and bookers for all they had done, sending them flowers and heartfelt notes. I really wanted them to know what a gift being a part of that world was for me.

Naturally, this is a very specific and personal example of how clothes empowered me as I was working to fulfill other important goals, but clothes can be relied upon to empower all of us in our everyday lives. I still rely on them to this day.

DRESSING FOR SUCCESS NOW

Of course, I cannot write a chapter on advocating for oneself through thoughtful grooming and appearance without talking about the dress code at Fox. It is very clearly a code based on honoring the value of the events we report and comment on. Fox News' philosophy extends to how we look as well as what we say. It also extends to men as well as women. *Everyone* at Fox is dressed as if they are representing the network—and the nation—because we are. Fox News is international. I truly share this conviction about showing your best self to the world every day, and I believe our viewers appreciate the extra effort we make too. (Many thanks to Gwen Marder, fashion director for Fox News, and the ladies in wardrobe; and to Jill Van Why, senior director of programming and production; along with our team in hair and makeup—the best in the business—for making the magic happen!)

The rules we follow are very specific. Our clothes are well tailored. The colors we wear are vibrant because television can't be static. Our hair is always styled and our makeup is impeccably applied too. There is great attention paid to detail.

It is understood that the quality and content of our work is our number one priority, but being put together really does complement and complete the whole message. There is no denying that Fox News features women of distinction and intelligence in all regards. Just think about it—Elisabeth Hasselbeck; Greta Van Susteren; Megyn Kelly; Jenna Lee; Gretchen Carlson; Anna Kooiman; Martha MacCallum; Lauren Green; Jamie Colby; Dagen McDowell; Elizabeth MacDonald; Gerri Willis; Deidre Bolton; Lori Rothman; Liz Claman; Lauren Simonetti; Claudia Cowan; Anita Vogel; Alicia Acuna; Carol Alt; Jennifer Griffin; Catherine Herridge; Molly Line; Juliet Huddy; Laura Ingle; Laura Ingraham; Angela McGlowan; Santita Jackson; Julie Roginsky; Jehmu Greene; Tamara Holder; Mercedes Colwin; KT McFarland; Arthel Neville; Lis Wiehl; Maria Bartiromo; Melissa Francis; Cheryl Casone; Uma Pemmaraju; Heather Nauert; Lea Gabrielle; Judge Jeanine Pirro; Julie Banderas; Shannon Bream; Heather Childers; Janice Dean; Maria Molina; and my cohost on *The Five*, Dana Perino, are just a few of the incredibly smart and talented women Fox has hired. On *Outnumbered*, on occasion I share the couch with many other amazing women, including Andrea Tantaros, Harris Faulkner, Sandra Smith, Kennedy, Ainsley Earhardt, Kirsten Powers, Katie Pavlich, Stacey Dash, Joanne Nosuchinsky, and Jedediah Bila. These are all hardworking ladies of depth and diverse experience who have made a commitment to paying attention to the whole self—*their exterior as well as their interior.* They are among the most talented women on television today, and I enjoy their company both on- and off-camera immensely.

Even if you don't place as high a value on appearance, you should know that it often affects salary. As unfair as that may be, it is a reality. Studies indicate that people's height, hair color, fitness, and even their tendency to wear makeup, among other factors, all have an impact on their pay. I'm not suggesting that you wear five-inch Louboutins and dye your hair blond or stop by Sephora or sign up for SoulCycle on your way home today, but I am telling you not to let a lack of attention to your appearance distract from your message. Even while she was fulfilling such an important role as secretary of state, people spent way too much time commenting on Hillary Clinton's pantsuits. How will you fare under similar scrutiny?

If you take just one piece of advice from me about the clothes you wear, it is this: when you get dressed each morning, remember that the way you look says something about you even at moments when you don't think you're being noticed or you didn't plan on making a case for yourself. *Whether you are aware of it or not, your appearance, along with your actions, builds the unspoken part of your case every day.*

For that reason alone, it's important to choose smart clothes.

I swear, there really is such a thing! We all know that wearing a tuxedo or an evening gown can make us feel more dashing or glamorous, so it stands to reason that dressing professionally can make us feel more polished too. Researchers at Northwestern's Kellogg School of Management have taken this thinking one step further. They've put forth a theory that what you wear not only makes a big impression on others, it makes a big impression on *you* as well—*one that is strong enough to improve your thought process and the quality of your work.* The theory is called "enclothed cognition." In the study, some of the subjects were asked to put on white coats while others were asked to look at white coats before participating in sustained attention tests. Some participants were told that the coats were lab coats, while others were told they were painters' smocks. Lab coats are universally associated with doctors, who by nature and training are very thorough and detail oriented. Interestingly enough, those thinking they were wearing a lab coat performed notably better than the other test groups, essentially exhibiting the same kind of focus and attention as medical professionals. These studies suggest that what we wear has the power to shape our thinking and abilities. *If you believed your choice of attire could have a positive impact on how well you did your job, and not just the way you appeared to others, wouldn't you make more conscious selections every morning?* At the very least, wouldn't you try out the theory on a day when you were making an important case? I know I'd choose smart clothes any day.

If you still don't have a clue what smart dressing is in your work environment, take a good look around you. During my early prosecutor days, it was pretty clear to me what was customary for lawyers to wear. Everyone suits up for a day in court. In television, it was instantly apparent that lively, monochromatic color plays a vital role in one's wardrobe choices as it can train the viewers' eyes on you. If you carefully scan the halls of your work environment, a pattern of acceptable and effective dress will emerge there too. Experts suggest that you check out what the people at the highest level are wearing. They're a good example of what to aim for. But if their style is unattainable due to cost, look to the rising stars in the levels just above you. You can pick up a number of useful cues from them. As you adapt to the culture around you, remember to still be your own person. You want to look like a member of the team, but you want your fans in upper management to be able to point you out as well.

It's also important to think about which fashions are likely to be long lasting and which might just be trends. Piercings and tattoos are more popular than ever, and they are a fantastic form of self-expression for many people. Your body, your life, your story, your history all have great value. Some people like to impress aspects of that onto themselves and carry it with them in a more significant and visible way. I'm all for that. Whatever helps you feel better and makes your life easier is fine with me. I certainly understand how having an inscription for a loved one you've lost can help you through that pain, or how commemorating a victory over a personal challenge can remind you to stay the course. I do, however, urge you to be thoughtful and contemplative about doing anything that is permanent in nature. *As with every action you intend to take, I'm suggesting that you present the best case you can to yourself before proceeding.* I don't want you to become paralyzed by the decision-making process, but I do want you to be sure that the choice you make now is one you can live with for the long term. Once you decide to proceed, keep to your decision. Commit and feel good about it.

While we're on the topic of appearances, let's address a few other factors that don't necessarily qualify as dress but definitely make

an impression on others. Listen up, recent grads, because a lot of
this applies to you. These tips are very specific lessons my father
taught me—lessons that I have built upon and am now passing
on to others.

My dad was a gentleman through and through. He was always
thoughtful and polite. He really believed in the importance of
manners. He also understood that the work force is filled with
people of all ages and social backgrounds, and that many people
with excellent social training expect others to have those same
graces too. So here's a gentle reminder to think more like someone
of his generation on occasion.

Definitely try to arrive a few minutes early to appointments
and on time for events you are invited to. Traffic jams are un-
avoidable, cabs are always scarce when you need them most, and
even the godsend that is Uber can't always ensure you'll get where
you're going on time, but make your best effort anyway. And remember the motto "better late than never." Don't bail out just
because you're running behind. Call or text ahead and keep those
you are meeting with informed.

It's also wise to behave *outside* of a meeting room the same way
you would *inside* a meeting room. This includes holding elevators
and doors open for other people. It's not as sexist as it sounds. You
should do this for anyone regardless of whether they are male,
female, members of senior management, or mailroom staff. It's a
really strong indication of your character. Also, be aware of who
you are sharing the corridors with and refrain from saying anything confidential or negative.

I shouldn't have to say this, but many people get so distracted
thinking about what they're going to say to the person they are
meeting with that they forget to be polite to the receptionist, assistant, and other support people who greet them. All of these
people play a vital role in the way things run in a work environ-

ment, even if that role is sometimes a less visible one. Everybody matters. They can be the biggest behind-the-scenes advocates you have. So don't just get your charm on for showtime. Make a great impression with the very first people you meet.

I also have a thing about introducing yourself and others properly, which I'm sure I learned from my dad as well. When you are meeting someone initially, say hello, extend a firm handshake, and be sure to tell them your complete name and the company you are with. It's nice to add that it's a pleasure to meet them. If you have already met them or you're not sure if you have, simply say "Nice to *see* you." Always introduce the others you are with too, and if your boss is in attendance, be sure to introduce her at the start.

One other platinum rule is to always be prepared. Certainly I mean mentally prepared, but I also mean physically prepared. Have copies of presentation materials ready in the preferred format—either as hard copies or as digital documents. Even if you sent the digital version in advance of your meeting, be sure to have it easily accessible to resend if you are asked to do so. This ensures that neither you nor the other party has to search through emails to find it again. If you are taking notes on your phone or iPad, it's also polite to let the other party know that is what you are doing so he doesn't think you're attending to other business while he talks.

Finally, please say thank you . . . and really mean it. Gratitude never goes out of style. Send a quick email after a meeting. The thought behind and immediate timing of your response is sometimes more effective than waiting to send a more formal handwritten note later.

All of this comes down to being your best, most cordial, and kind self at all times. Self-advocating is a lot like being an ambassador. Every sincere and positive gesture advances your relationship with those around you and affirms that you are someone they can place their trust and confidence in when new opportunities arise.

CHAPTER 3

Asking for a Promotion

You now know how to interview to get the job you want. You know how to dress to continue to make the best impression possible. You even learned how to keep your job or move on with dignity when circumstances arise that are beyond your control. *So how do you advocate for that promotion you so richly deserve after putting in the time?*

While getting that coveted new position can be challenging at times, it is not impossible. Luckily there are ways to be successful at seeking, creating, and securing better-paying and more challenging opportunities for yourself, both within your company and outside of it too. As always, it all hinges on making your case.

At this point I could simply suggest that you follow all the suggestions laid out for you in chapters 1 and 2, since getting a promotion is fundamentally the same as getting any other job.

But there is a nuanced aspect to your approach that can really make a difference, whether you are pursuing an existing job at a higher level or you are pitching new positions expressly created for you as more and more people are doing. It starts with a set of tools I keep sharpened every day.

By now, you all know that I'm a planner. And planners by nature are master list makers. I keep a daily calendar, where I note all of the things I want to accomplish on a given day and I delete tasks from the list as they are completed. I really believe that lists help you identify, focus on, and achieve your goals one step at a time. Being productive is rewarding in the moment and in the long run too.

What I love most about lists, though, is that they can make you a more logical thinker and an infinitely better communicator. I've always known the importance of language and have made it a habit to contemplate what I'm going to say before I say it so I don't deliver my message in the wrong way. Lists have been a tremendous aid in preparing myself throughout my legal and television careers. They help crystallize my talking points so I can make my case as directly as possible, whenever or wherever I need to. My great friend and cohost Dana Perino is a list maker too. Having this quality has been incredibly valuable to her as an on- and off-air communications expert and certainly as a former White House press secretary, where she had to speak on behalf of the president. Is there any more important communication job than that?

I also find that lists enhance my resolve. When I write out my goals, a visual and mental connection forms that somehow deepens my commitment to making things happen. It's as if I'm calling on my senses to witness my determination and to act as reinforcements to help get the job done.

People who don't take the time to make lists or plan often say that they prefer to be spontaneous. Many see themselves as greater risk takers. But I don't believe these qualities are mutually exclusive. As it happens, planning not only helps me spot opportunities more readily, it also enables me to jump on and make the most of those opportunities.

If you don't believe me, just ask Henry Schleiff, head of Court TV. While my first husband, Gavin Newsom, was mayor of San Francisco, I decided to take a leave of absence from the DA's office to avoid any potential conflicts of interest or suggestion of impropriety. During that time, various news programs asked me to serve as a legal analyst. I was in New York one day in that capacity, scheduled to appear on *Catherine Crier,* when the lights went out. It was a hot August afternoon so the air conditioners were on full blast. I thought the problem was due to the heat and that it would be resolved quickly. Instead, it turned out to be a widespread power outage that lasted for days throughout parts of the northeastern and midwestern United States and in Ontario, Canada, but I didn't know that at the time. I was there to do a job and I was going to do it no matter what. Without traffic lights, the streets were jammed with cars going nowhere fast, so getting a cab was impossible. I decided to walk the thirty blocks to the studio. That's what you would do, right? Most people were fleeing while I was making a beeline for the chairman and CEO's office. My first stop was the secretary's desk, the gatekeeper. I introduced myself and explained that I was in town from San Francisco and only needed a few minutes of Mr. Schleiff's time to say hi. I was selling it. As it turned out only upper management—Mr. Schleiff, Art Bell, and Marlene Dann—were still there. I knew this was my chance. I thought to myself, "Time to check the box. The decision makers are still in the building." I was led down the corridor to a big corner office. It was dark, but there was still some natural light streaming in through the windows, so I stayed a while to talk with Mr. Schleiff. My friend Rikki Klieman was Court TV's legal analyst at the time and host of *Both Sides*. I'm not sure how the subject came up, but we began to talk about how Rikki and her husband, Bill Bratton, who was New York City's chief of police at the time, were planning on making a move to LA. (They have since returned to New York and he is once again the city's police commissioner.) Of course, I instantly started to pitch myself for Rikki's soon-to-be-vacant position. I said, "Let me tell you something. Look no further. I am the best choice to host this show. I'm your girl and here's why." I gave him my most convincing list of reasons and then closed with my classic line, "Offer me the job—I'll give you your money back if you're disappointed." He made the offer and the rest is history as they say. When interviewed about it later, Henry joked that he was afraid *not* to hire me. I basically sat down in the middle of a major blackout, undaunted by the dark, and made my case because it seemed to me that there was no better time or place, or more captive an audience.

The only way I can explain this event is to say that there are occasions when you have to make your own luck, and occasions when something is right there in front of you waiting for you to pounce. In the latter situation you can't just say, "Oh wait, whoa. I have to think about this." You have to be ready and you have to be able to make the decision to go for it without any hesitation. Planning makes you agile enough to do that. When you're a planner, your goals are always fresh in your mind. You can say why you're the right person for the job without skipping a beat. My story proves that. So think ahead. *And be fearless.*

I find it sad that people spend more time planning meals, vacations, what to wear, or the perfect get-together with friends than they do planning to meet their goals. Now that you understand the importance of this step, I know you'll invest the time to always plan as you move forward. It really does prepare you for every eventuality and can even invite more spontaneity into your life.

In addition to planning and making lists, here are a few other suggestions to help you make a powerful case for getting your next promotion:

- It is imperative that you be aware of your environment. Always consider where you are. Are you in an office or in a noisy restaurant? Is there privacy? Or are there too many opportunities for interruptions? You want to be sure that when you make your pitch you will have the other party's undivided attention.

- The same is true for timing. It's always wise to take a temperature reading before scheduling an appointment or speaking up spontaneously. Being aware of other people's emotions or having a sense of what is happening on that particular day can make a real difference in the outcome of your conversation. People will be more or less receptive to your request depending upon when you ask, so always be careful to read the cues. Oddly enough, pitching in the midst of a blackout proved to be excellent timing *and* an excellent choice of place for me. The studio was quiet; there were virtually no other distractions. Henry and I hit it off right away. He was my kind of people. It was great getting to know each other. I thanked him for his time—remember, don't talk past the sale. When I left the room I *knew* I had the job.

• It's also crucial to be aware of your boss or interviewer's preferred style of communication. If your boss is the type of person who doesn't like a lot of small talk, be prepared; write down what you want to say; think economy of words; make your case in three points; and *boom*, be on your way. Don't be verbose. My brother uses the phrase *no unnecessary conversation*. So if you work for people like him, just cut to the chase. Having respect for their time will increase their respect for you.

• You should also be mindful of your own style. Again, I must refer to the brilliant Roger Ailes and a book he wrote titled *You Are the Message*, which I have read many, many times over the years. I even brought my dog-eared copy of it with me on my first interview with him so he could sign it. As fate would have it, it was the assigned reading for my public speaking class at UC Davis. In its chapters, he explains that your voice, tone, volume, gestures, and the overall energy you bring to your message say as much about you as the words you choose to speak. Of course, your wit and charm count heavily too. All of these things, collectively and apart, signal to people what kind of person you are. They reveal your authentic character, passion and commitment, and, in this case, what kind of job you'll do. Don't be afraid to use all of these tools. They are already at your disposal. Make it clear that you want and can do this job—not just with your words, but with your body language too. *Sell it.*

- One more thing: when it comes time to talking about money, be prepared.

NEGOTIATING YOUR SALARY

. . . .

Show me the money. How you negotiate your salary sends a strong message to your employer about how you negotiate on behalf of the company in your day-to-day business, so this is the time to shine. In addition to coming to the table armed with the facts about how you are perfect for the new position or why you deserve a raise, it's a good idea to know what other companies in the industry are paying people in comparable positions. When negotiating a contract with an outside vendor for your company, you research what the going rate for similar services are, right? Well the same logic applies when you are negotiating for your own fair compensation. You need to know what the going rate for *your* services are, and the way to do that is to get comps. It's just like when you are buying or selling a house and you want to know if the asking price is within range.

These days, it's really not that hard to find this information. There are so many excellent resources online; you no longer have to be an investigative journalist to figure out what other people are earning. There are sites designed specifically to help you calculate your worth. Many offer salary information across all industries and break down the information by company size and location. A few even let you customize your search according to years of experience, education, and other specific factors. Some also provide data on overtime, bonuses, commissions, and profit shares, as well as gratuities for those of you in the service industry. A few of the popular resources for this information include CareerBuilder.com, Simplyhired.com, Monster.Salary.com, Glassdoor.com, Beyond .com, Payscale.com, Salary.com, SalaryExpert.com, Indeed.com, CareerBliss.com, and JobSearchIntelligence.com.

Once you have a relative idea of what your salary range should be, you can approach the discussion of compensation with as much clarity as you'd discuss fees with any new vendor—only this time you will be pursuing the best deal you can get on behalf of *yourself.* See what your employer is offering first. You don't want to be the one to throw out the initial number on the off chance they were prepared to pay you more. If you're not happy with the amount they quote, don't be afraid to put the figure you have in mind out there. Since you've done your research it won't be out of line.

Ladies, studies show that men do this all the time. They ask for raises more frequently than we do and they don't hesitate to negotiate, whether it's for their starting salary, annual increase, or a promotion. Among the 1,500 women interviewed as part of an ivillage.com survey conducted in 2013, only 35 percent said they had ever asked for a raise. Many women fear that contesting their salary will cost them their jobs, and certainly that is understandable. The other factor that may be discouraging females from speaking up is all the talk we hear about the gender wage gap. It can make some women feel as if the pursuit of a higher salary is futile. However, many of you are under a misimpression. The Department of Labor tells us that women earn $.77 for every dollar a man earns, but according to the Independent Women's Forum, more recent data tells us the figure is actually $.82 for every dollar. And when economist June O'Neill examined the numbers, taking into consideration experience, career choice, time out of the workforce, and education, the gap was just 3.3 percent, with women earning $.97 for every dollar a man earns. This is encouraging news for women, but the larger point is that no matter what the prevailing conditions are, getting what we deserve rests on how convincing a case we make for ourselves, so do your research, know your value, and build the best case you can based upon that information. There are some people who would like to broaden the laws protecting equal pay even more in an effort to close what they believe is a wider pay gap, but I don't think you should abdicate greater control to the government. While it would make it easier to sue companies for wage disparities that occurred a long time ago, this will only cost companies more money in legal fees and back pay, which will result in less hiring and lower wages overall. It is up to you to fight for comparable pay every time you apply for a new job or have a performance review. And remember, one way to build your case is to include examples of how you have and will continue to work well with others to achieve the company's goals. This is one of female workers' greatest strengths. And since discussing compensation often makes employer and employee feel like they are on opposing sides in a championship game, taking this tact should help remind everyone that you're a team player going for the same team win.

If, however, at the end of presenting a solid case for yourself, your employer has valid reasons for not meeting your salary demand (I'm a realist after all—that can and does happen), then you can choose to accept or decline their offer accordingly. I hope your employer would respect you for at least having stated your case and explored the possibilities. You can always remind her that you approach your work with the same kind of moxie as you approached this negotiation. If her reasons do, in fact, have more to do with the company's economics than your performance, think about asking for some other accommodations. Could a six-month review to reevaluate both the climate and your accomplishments in that time be arranged? Or could you be given a performance bonus at the end of the year equal to the difference in what you asked for and what they offered, provided you meet certain preset goals? *As always, when making an effective case, state your position fully and clearly, genuinely listen to the response, respectfully counter their objections with the intent of persuading them with further facts, and/or propose a common ground solution.*

I know that for some of you negotiating for yourself will take practice, but no matter what the outcome on your first try, take pride in the fact that you just played by one of my dad's top rules. He always encouraged me to take risks and to go after what I wanted because he thought that was among the best ways to guarantee that I never looked back and wondered, *What if?* Of course, he warned me to proceed with my eyes wide open so I could time those risks for when the circumstances were most favorable, but he never wanted me to avoid a challenge—even one as tough as asking for more money—because I was worried about failing or being denied. If that ever happened, he'd simply tell me to try harder next time.

My dad also taught me another relevant lesson: *promotions are not just for work.* A promotion means to raise yourself up, so I try to do that in other parts of my life too. In addition to setting goals for what I want to do on the job or in my long-term career, I make lists of goals for my personal relationships and with regard to my personal finance, health, physical fitness, and spiritual and community life. When you are happy in all these areas, you will find that you have and convey a stronger sense of self and confidence at work.

CHAPTER 4

Standing Up for Your Ideas

There are people to this day who observe how determined I can be and say, "Kimberly, you can't *will* everything." But honestly, I don't accept that. I truly believe that if there is a will there is a way.

One of the leaders I still admire most was the great communicator, Ronald Reagan. I loved the way he built and framed his message. He used eloquence, humor, and common sense to great effect. (Traits I should add to every list of dos in this book.) I find the themes of his presidency relevant even today. During his State of the Union address in 1985 he reminded us that "There are no constraints on the human mind, no walls around the human spirit, no barriers to our progress except those we ourselves erect." He was a leader who questioned and changed the established way of doing things and who encouraged us to do the same as citizens of a free country. His message was always clear and consistent. Especially in matters of economic growth and security, he wanted us to be a take-charge nation—to be a people more responsible and accountable for our own destiny.

The best example of being responsible and accountable for your own destiny, of course, is to make your case—and to live by its twin tenet: stand up for your ideas. I remember doing that in a very big way when my television career was just taking off, and before that, during one of the last cases I tried.

It was when Gavin was mayor and I took a formal leave of absence from the DA's office. Shortly before, I had tried a case that was one of the most publicized in San Francisco history. In fact, it had made international headlines. As a result of this case and subsequent media I had done, I received a lot of interest from news and opinion shows to provide on-air legal analysis of other popular cases. Dan Abrams not only reached out to me frequently when he was covering that case for NBC/MSNBC on site in Los Angeles, but he also was the very first person to book me as a legal analyst on his prime-time show *The Abrams Report*. In that way, he was instrumental in starting my television career.

I ended up getting offers from ABC News, *Good Morning America*, Court TV, Fox News, CNN, and MSNBC. I was flattered by all of the generous offers I received and I wanted to figure out a way to accept more than one. I believe in having multiple revenue streams and being recession-proof. But my agent at the time was opposed to me accepting more than a single offer. I believe his words were "It just isn't done." To which I quickly replied, "Why not?" I was determined to find a way to at least give exclusivity to a different party in different time slots. And so we made it work. Being told that no one has ever worked for more than one network at a time just wasn't a good enough reason for me. I asked my agent to tell them that if they were dissatisfied with my performance and availability they could most certainly have their money back.

Although Fox had offered me a position as a legal analyst, it required total exclusivity and I was concerned that would prevent me from taking any of the other positions. In the end I worked it out so that I was on ABC in the morning from 9:00 am until after the West Coast re-airs were done, usually around noon. That left me free to do my Court TV show called *Both Sides* between 1:00 pm and 3:00 pm. I was also exclusive to CNN for prime time, working for both Anderson Cooper at 7:00 pm and Larry King at 9:00 pm. I had the whole day and evening of news covered. I am immeasurably grateful to Anderson Cooper and Larry King for their support and to everyone who worked with me to help make this happen.

My agent was right about one thing—to the best of my knowledge nothing like that had ever been done before with multiple paid positions. I took charge of my own destiny and actually started a trend that worked really well for me and is now an option for others. Just because something is difficult doesn't mean it's impossible. I stood up for my ideas and more important, I found a way to make them happen. I will not be regulated by anyone else's unwritten laws or by common practice. *I will always question whether the way things work is the best way possible and if not, figure out how it can work better for me and others with similar goals.* You should stand up for your ideas too—and for the ideas of others you agree with as well. And you should see them to fruition. All too often people fail to execute the ideas they fought for. Don't be that person. It makes fighting for the next goal with the same party so much harder. Be the type of person who actively stands behind your words.

Of course, there are many examples of my colleagues and me standing up for our ideas during my California court days. If there weren't, none of us would ever have become DAs. But there were two especially notable situations that should be mentioned here. One involved the famous case I briefly mentioned earlier.

In 2001, my colleague James Hammer and I prosecuted Robert Noel and Marjorie Knoller in the dog-mauling death of a thirty-three-year-old lacrosse coach named Diane Whipple. The case made headlines because of the horrific nature of the attack and because of the severity of the charges we were pursuing against the defendants. The dogs involved in the crime had originally been purchased by Paul Schneider, a high-ranking member of the prison gang the Aryan Brotherhood. While Schneider was serving a life sentence without parole in the maximum-security Pelican Bay State Prison for prior criminal offenses, he and his cellmate Dale Bretches, who was also serving a life term, attempted to start an illegal Internet dog-fighting business called Dog-O'-War. The business sought to breed and sell a type of dog known as Presa Canarios. After we issued search warrants for Schneider and Bretches's cell, further evidence was found indicating that the two also planned to sell these violent dogs to the Mexican mafia to guard methamphetamine labs being run in Southern California. Originally, Presa Canarios served as cattle herders and protection dogs on the Canary Islands off Spain, but due to their genetically high prey drive, they began more recently to be developed for use in blood sport and were first imported to the United States for this purpose in 1990.

A fifty-year-old woman named Janet Coumbs, who had been visiting Schneider in prison as part of her Christian ministry, naively agreed to keep the dogs Schneider purchased for his business chained up on a remote part of her farm in Trinity County, California, until they and/or their puppies could be sold. Unfortunately, two of the dogs, Bane and Hera, became increasingly aggressive to the point that Coumbs could no longer handle the animals. They terrorized everyone on the farm, had killed a cat and several sheep, and had done incredible damage to a building on the property. Noel and Knoller, who were Schneider's lawyers at the time, ultimately brought Hera, and then Bane, into their one-bedroom San Francisco apartment down the hall from Whipple's. Because neither dog received early socialization or proper obedience training before being introduced to this more populated area, they became even more of a threat than they had been on the farm. Despite having been warned in writing by a veterinarian who examined the dogs, by Coumbs, and by victims who previously had been lunged at or bitten by these two dogs in thirty other alleged incidents (one involving a pregnant woman and another involving a six-year-old boy), the defendants failed to take sufficient precautions against the future harm of innocent people.

Prior to the case, the mischievous dog statute in the State of California (section 399 of the penal code) only held "owners" and persons having "control or custody of a dog" liable for criminal negligence when a dog attack resulted in the death or injury of a human. If Jim and I had not appealed to and testified before the State Assembly to have the code changed to also include "persons who control and are responsible for the dog but do not have title," the crime could not have been tried as a felony. It is very likely that the case would have been tried as a misdemeanor or as a mere infraction, resulting in only a three-year suspension of the couple's dog-ownership privileges. It was clear to us from the evidence that was gathered that Noel and Knoller knew the risks of keeping these dogs in a domestic environment, and they blatantly ignored those risks. They fit all the criteria except that they technically were not the owners. Their lack of control over dogs that repeatedly attacked or threatened others demonstrated a wanton disregard for human life. Jim and I were adamant that this case, and others like it, had to be tried as a felony for justice to be served and that is exactly what happened. The murder of Diane Whipple was a vicious, heinous, and senseless act that never should have occurred. We invoked the law of implied malice murder, with the understanding that malice can be based simply on a defendant's conscious disregard of the risk of serious bodily injury (not only on conscious disregard of the risk of death). In the end, both defendants were found guilty of involuntary manslaughter and owning a mischievous animal that caused the death of another human being. Knoller, who was present at the attack and did little to try to stop it—even leaving the scene of the crime at one point—was found guilty of the additional and more serious charge of second-degree murder and sentenced to fifteen years in prison. The convictions and sentencing in this precedent-setting case were later upheld by the Supreme Court of California, the state's highest court.

I cannot possibly overstate the importance of this verdict as the ownership and mishandling of breeds with violent tendencies in populated areas was on a very sharp rise at the time, as was the underground organized crime of dogfighting. While prosecuting cases in LA prior to returning to San Francisco, I had witnessed firsthand just how rampant the problem was. I saw what these devastating kinds of attacks did to the victims physically, mentally, emotionally, and financially. I also saw how damaging the whole practice is to the poor animals engaged in fighting. But don't just take my word for it. The Humane Society of the United States estimates that there are at least forty thousand dogfighters in America. Interestingly enough, as the presence of these superbreeds increased, our country began to experience a dog-bite epidemic. From 1986–1996, the nation's dog population rose by

only 2 percent, yet the number of bites requiring medical attention increased by 33 percent. According to current data from the
Centers for Disease Control and Prevention, nearly 4.5 million
Americans are bitten by dogs each year. More than 885,000 of
those victims need treatment for their wounds and as many as
27,000 must endure reconstructive surgery. The Noel and Knoller case not only ended with a just verdict, but it also heightened
awareness of this growing problem. It was an important stand
for us to take. I'm proud that we did what we believed was right,
and that I still continue to speak up on principle in my life today.
Props to Jim Hammer who is a great prosecutor and friend, and
who was the head of the homicide unit at the San Francisco district attorney's office at the time.

As you can see, I'm never afraid to initiate change or to buck
convention if the situation warrants it. There have been others
before me who have inspired me to be fearless in that way. For
instance, I vividly recall the very first time I watched my former
boss and mentor Stephen Kay try a case. He interacted with the
jury in such a real and authentic way. I had to know how he
was doing it. I soon realized that he was speaking with them so
effectively because he was working without note cards. You have
to understand that this too was something that just wasn't done.
Every prosecutor I know wants to have full command over the
facts of an argument when they are addressing the jury because
the stakes are so high. Having note cards ensures that the facts are
at their fingertips when they are not yet on the tip of their tongue.
But Stephen memorizes his notes and goes in boldly without
them because he truly believes that it's crucial to know your facts
and to connect with the jury face-to-face when addressing them.
When he locks eyes with them, he's making the members of this
twelve-person team individually accountable for listening carefully and for thinking about all the information he is presenting.

He knows the benefits of doing this are enormous. He studies the facts until he can repeat them like they are his own personal history. He taught me to do the same with my closing arguments. He would always say, "It's in you. Rely on yourself. You've got the means. You know the case. Trust yourself." And he was right. By the time you are ready to try a case the details are lodged in your bones. Because I did trust myself, the jury trusted me too. It all comes down to this: when our job of building and presenting a case is done, the responsibility of arriving at a final verdict rests with the jurors. Looking at each one eye-to-eye is a really personal way of passing the baton to them—of encouraging them to put time and thought into reaching a fair and just conclusion in the same way that we put the time and energy into gathering and presenting the evidence. I want to make my jurors feel like they have skin in the game. That they are part of this. I want them fully invested. Talking to them in this way is an invitation for them to be take-charge and responsible citizens. The kind of citizen former president Reagan knew we all have the potential to be. *Attorneys are frequently reminded in the course of their work that we really do have the freedom to stand up for our ideas in this country, and I for one never take that freedom for granted.* I exercise that freedom at home, with friends, on Twitter, and now in the court of popular opinion. You can too. You never know how you can have an impact on the world with your ideas until you are willing to build your case for them, fight for them, and truly act on them.

When gathering the resolve to stand up for your ideas, remember:

People who speak their mind effectively, *know* their own mind. They are in touch with their views because they take the time to be alone with their thoughts. They think through all sides of an argument and have considered the potential impact before speaking.

They have great passion, but are always guided by the facts more than by emotions. They do the research to back their views and always have that research at their command. They take risks, but they rarely see them as such because they know they are armed with a compelling argument.

They never worry about what other people think of them. They don't seek approval so much as they seek change or progress.

They persist under all circumstances. If at first they don't succeed at making their case, they appeal. They pursue alternate ways, times, and places to state their views until they are heard.

My dad would also add that they are people who know *listening is a powerful statement too.* He'd urge my brother and me to truly hear what others have to say before and after speaking. He reminded us often that when you put your opinions out there, they are bound to be met by criticism and opposing viewpoints. If you respect the good that speaking up promotes, then you will listen to the other side and weigh the pros and cons of what they have to say in the same way you hope they will for you. It all comes down to respecting your opponent's right to speak out as well. But opposing views don't have to stifle you. I think my dad would love the fact that today I am on several shows where opposing viewpoints are welcome and hashed out together.

CHAPTER 5

Working as a Team

I 've always been a big fan of team sports. You've already heard about my soccer and softball exploits, and certainly you know that if you spent any time in my house when I was growing up, you were automatically a member of Team Guilfoyle. The circumstances of my childhood fostered an all-for-one-one-for-all attitude.

That kind of upbringing taught me a valuable lesson: when a team plays well together they propel *everyone* forward. Sometimes advocating for yourself or a cause can be a lot like playing for a team. You can get a lot further if you have people with different strengths, skills, and perspectives on your side working in sync toward a common goal. Your assessment of the odds and your efforts to beat those odds can be so much more comprehensive that way. I've been very lucky throughout my career to have always worked alongside colleagues with complementary talents and the kind of superstrong team spirit that helps us all meet our objectives.

After I graduated from college I was a teacher for a while, just like my mom. Teachers are the ultimate team players, often working together across different disciplines to advocate for their students' academic and social growth. Prosecuting attorneys also work in teams. The fate of an individual is too important to rest in only one person's hands. It's why we have juries of twelve people as well. And, of course, on *The Five* and *Outnumbered* I am part of an incredible team of cohosts who together are able to cover a wider range of topics and offer more well-rounded opinions than any one of us could alone. Since I've already talked about the dynamic ladies on *Outnumbered*, let me tell you a little bit about the team that is *The Five*.

I love working with Dana Perino, Eric Bolling, Greg Gutfeld, and Bob Beckel, and I also enjoy working with Andrea Tantaros and Juan Williams, who launched the show with us and who still join us from time to time. Andrea now cohosts the new FNC show *Outnumbered* and Juan is a regular panelist on *Fox News Sunday* and *Special Report with Bret Baier*. He is also a regular substitute host for *The O'Reilly Factor*.

Fox and *The Five* is like home to me. My colleagues are more than team players; they are family. They've all made my life larger, fuller, richer. We're a superclose group. Best friends, really. I also love working with these amazing people because each has mastered the art of advocacy in different ways that I admire and respect.

Dana Perino and I are particularly close. We're both transplants to New York—she came from Washington, D.C., and I came from the West Coast. Although we've been here for quite a while, we still love to explore the city together. We live in the same neighborhood and I always follow her recommendations for great places to try. Recently we went on a girls date after work and she took me on the subway to show me how to get home. Like a real New Yorker, she had changed into sensible shoes while I was still wearing five-inch heels. It was very funny. I learned my lesson. She's an incredibly thoughtful friend— an avid reader who is always finding and sending me articles related to all the things she knows I'm interested in. Just about every morning she sends me a photo of her dog Jasper doing something that makes us both laugh. I treasure the relationship I have with Dana and her husband, Peter. He is one of the funniest guys I've ever met. When the chips are down they are a couple you know you can count on. Most fans of the show know that Dana loves animals, but I'm not sure they know that she helps to pair rescue dogs with veterans suffering from PTSD through an organization called Companion Heroes. She always extends her reach as far as it can go. What I love most about Dana is that she brings a certain fearlessness to the table. As someone who was once the spokesperson for POTUS (while we were at war no less), she knows how to handle herself under the most stressful of circumstances. And having worked for the Justice Department and the Council on Environmental Policy she also knows a lot about advocacy. She can always be relied upon to say what other people are thinking but don't necessarily have the right words or courage to say themselves. And she does it with a kind of rational calm viewers and I really appreciate. Those are among the best advocacy skills anyone can have. Her fans will also be thrilled that she's sharing even more of her wisdom in her recently published book, *And the Good News Is . . . : Lessons and Advice from the Bright Side.*

Greg Gutfeld is my buddy. We go way back to the days when his show *Red Eye* first started and I was a regular on it. In fact, he was the one who first began calling me KG on air. He's *such* a funny guy. He's a world-class advocate too, who uses one of my favorite advocacy tools of all time—humor. No one in television today has a voice quite like his. He has a unique point of view and delivery style. One of the things that makes him so interesting is that he is wildly unpredictable. I always look forward to hearing his monologue and his fresh take on the news of the day. He's daring and irreverent in a very intellectual way. You could be listening to news for hours, but at 5:00 pm you know you're going to get something different. As a satirist, he can incite or defuse a riot at will. He can make a divisive statement and then bring us all together by making us laugh over it. He not only does this nightly on *The Five*, but he also does it on *Red Eye*, where he is so likable that people who disagree with him still take his comments in stride the way they'd take the comments of their most headstrong friend. He is a perfectionist with a great command of language. Having been a *New York Times* bestselling author, blogger, and editor for countless online and print publications, including *Prevention*, *Men's Health*, *The Huffington Post*, and his own blog, *The Daily Gut*, among others, he speaks off the cuff as impressively as he writes.

Eric Bolling is like a big brother to me. I really enjoy spending time with him and his lovely wife, Adrienne. I admire their relationship and the partnership they have together. They're so much fun. They really know how to enjoy life. They work hard, yet they still make time for each other and their son, Eric Chase. Eric and I go way back too. We worked together on *Follow the Money* on the Fox Business Network and *The Strategy Room* on Fox News .com, where we developed a great rapport.

You'd never know it to see his success today, but Eric grew up poor in inner city Chicago. He had loving parents who supported his passion for sports. He pursued a career in baseball after receiving a great education that included a fellowship at Duke University's Public Policy Graduate Program. He was then drafted by the

Pittsburgh Pirates, but suffered a career-ending rotator cuff injury. But that didn't stop him. He went on to build one of the world's top oil and gas trading companies. He was elected to the board of directors of The New York Mercantile Exchange where he drove the company to one of the largest IPOs at the time. CNBC soon recruited him for their new show *Fast Money*. He then came to Fox. Although he doesn't play ball anymore, *The Five* still provides an opportunity for him to go to bat for the things he believes in. The advocacy skill I like most about Eric is that he's a high-energy guy who remains incredibly upbeat in all circumstances. To get what you want in life you need to maintain optimism.

On many levels, Bob is the one who has to advocate the hardest on our show, since he's the one who most often holds opposing viewpoints, but I love that he is never daunted by that fact. He is always up for the fight. He says what he thinks and isn't deterred by anyone. He's also had a stellar career as an advocate. He worked on Robert F. Kennedy's presidential campaign while in college. He served as the nation's youngest deputy assistant secretary of state during the Carter administration. He was also the national campaign manager for Walter Mondale's 1984 presidential bid. The advocacy traits he exhibits are, of course, an abundance of unrelenting passion and feistiness. I know he comes off as a liberal attack dog on the show, but I think that's largely because when you run campaigns for a living, you're always fighting for ground. You've got to be scrappy. What may not always show through is how gentle and kindhearted Bob is to us off camera. He has a real sensitive side and a heart of gold. He always asks me how my son is doing. He has a real fondness for Ronan. He likes to talk politics with him—Bob will do anything to get a vote! I remember when Ronan had his tonsils taken out, Bob, as part of the whole Fox family, sent a bunch of different flavored Graeter's ice creams to lift his spirits. It was just what the doctor ordered.

A good advocate can adamantly disagree with your views but will always remember to treat you with compassion just the same.

Andrea Tantaros and I became friends when I first joined Fox. We bonded over our close relationship with our fathers. She was with me moments after I learned that my dad's condition had taken a turn for the worse and I had to fly home immediately. She comforted me and later told me she was so upset she called her own father to remind him of how much she loved him. Little did she know then that her dad would also be stricken with cancer and would pass away just one year later. This forged a lasting connection between us that has only deepened over the years. She is loyal and she is strong. Her confidence is one of her best advocacy traits. It comes, in part, from how well she prepares. Her political analysis is always spot on and she never shies away from a good fight. Even before appearing on *The Five*, this trait was evident when she and Bob would battle it out on *America's Newsroom*. The two of them have this great on-air chemistry—they'd clash but always remain friends.

Juan Williams is one of my most inspirational friends. He's a master of both the spoken and the written word, having spent more than ten years with NPR, where he served as a senior national correspondent and news analyst, and twenty-three years at *The Washington Post*. He's won many awards for his writing and investigative journalism, as well as an Emmy Award for television documentary writing. Somehow he has found the time to pen numerous magazine articles and to author six books as well, including the nonfiction bestseller *Eyes on the Prize: America's Civil Rights Years, 1954–1965* and *Thurgood Marshall: American Revolutionary*. He's been tenacious throughout his career. I particularly admire his advocacy for school choice and his recent challenge to President Obama and other Democrats to stop favoring unions and start favoring our kids by improving the qual-

ity and number of options for those who want the best education
for their children that they can get. There is no better advocacy
tool than a great education, and he is fighting to put that useful
tool within every child's reach.

The day I began writing this chapter, I took a step back and
really observed all of us in the studio. Before the show began,
Greg was jazzed about what he wanted to say in the first segment. He was on a tear about the media abdicating its role during
the spate of scandals the White House has faced since President
Obama has been in office. He shared a few of his top points with
Dana and there was the usual supportive banter back and forth.
We really do value one another's opinions and feedback. During
those few moments before we go live it's not uncommon for us to
run thoughts by each other, and we touch base throughout the
day as stories are developing. Eric came in, trimming copy down
to the most cogent lines right up to the very last minute. He's a
perfectionist that way. On that same evening, Bob cut it close
twice when we were on air, nearly using the kind of colorful language we're told to be on guard against whenever we get in heated
discussions. I can usually help cut the tension with a joke or two
during the breaks when things like that happen, as I did then.
That's how we roll. There has to be static electricity sometimes
for us to be able to catch lightning in a bottle as often as we do. It
goes with the territory.

I think the reason our show appeals to so many people is that
what you see on the show is very real. We're people who deeply
care about the times and the events unfolding in the world we live
in and we care for one another. We'd even go so far as to save one
another's lives, which Eric did once when he prevented Bob from
choking on a shrimp at lunch by using the Heimlich maneuver.
True story! We are like lively, opinionated relatives sitting around
the table at dinnertime—just like our viewers are—talking about

the things that are on everyone's mind. We can get riled up. There are moments when we have absolutely no filters. We push one another's buttons, and sometimes we just have to agree to disagree. But we all have our say and in the end, we always have a good time with one another because we have mutual respect, and we are all doing what we love and what we think serves a larger purpose. We each bring something different to the debate and as a result we resonate with a much wider audience. *If there ever were a time when I didn't agree with a single person at that table it would probably frustrate me, but it would be okay because the thing we all have in common is that we are advocates for ideas, and the object of our working together as a team is to protect and exercise the right to express those ideas even when they are different.* In that regard, we make a great team *and* we make great advocates.

Your job, whether you realize it or not, is a lot like mine. You navigate through different opinions, work styles, and views because for the most part, your boss, colleagues, employees, and you share many common interests and goals. You all gravitated to the same industry, the same company, and the same department hoping to make a difference in your field and the world, aware that you can do that better in numbers than individually. Even though you may have your own personal goals, you were all hired to work together to advance the common company goals. Finding that thing that makes you an asset to the team—the thing that helps round out the group's collective abilities—is how you promote yourself and them at the same time. It's how you become an advocate and a team player at once. *Advocating for yourself, in the broadest terms, is really finding your place in the world. Since that's such a tall order, we find our place in one group at a time.* We do what we do best in that group, develop some new skills, and after growing and evolving as much as we can, we often graduate to a larger group or expand our role within the current one.

Expanding that role may even mean becoming a team leader, a manager, and, in a way, an uber-advocate—someone who more formally mobilizes, organizes, motivates, and incentivizes other team members and the group as a whole. I found that role rewarding when I was a prosecutor and I took it very seriously too. I was in charge of supervising the police and directing their investigations as they pertained to my cases. I also headed up the training division for new prosecutors. All the members of my team were professional and diligent people, but I would also put 110 percent effort into the job as a means of leading by example. What I found is that people respect and work harder for you when they see that you hold the same high standards for yourself as you do for them. No matter how many people work for or with you, you cannot consistently get good results unless you are also willing to put in the same time and effort, or more. Leaders, in many ways, are just more intense team players. I continue to see examples of this every day. Two leaders at Fox come to mind.

The first is Bill O'Reilly. Every week my friend Lis Wiehl and I appear on a popular segment of *The O'Reilly Factor* called "Is It Legal?" I'm incredibly grateful to Bill for giving me a chance to showcase all that I learned in my years as a prosecutor. But just as important, I'm grateful for the opportunity to watch and learn from one of the smartest, most focused, most talented, and hardest-working men in television. Bill not only has an excellent sense of story selection and an extraordinary ability to connect with the viewing audience, but he also works more intensely than anyone else on his team or anyone else I know, for that matter. He decides every aspect of the program, large and small. It's one of the reasons it's been so successful for so long. He is extremely hands-on and his attention to detail is unparalleled in the industry. He sets the bar high for those who work with him, but it's great fun rising to meet his challenge.

I also have the distinct pleasure of being on Sean Hannity's show. Sean believed in me from day one. Despite the fact that he is a huge prime-time star and has evolved into one of the most compelling voices on television and radio, he still works hard and treats everybody around him with such respect and appreciation. He is the nicest guy. He always remembers his humble roots, which not only makes him a great team leader but also a great family man and someone I truly admire.

I value team spirit so much, in fact, I keep a list of attributes that all great team players and team advocates should have. I review it from time to time when I'm in need of inspiration or a quick pep talk. I am sharing it with you now in the hope that following this list will help you become a better advocate too.

- **GREAT TEAM PLAYERS/ADVOCATES COMMIT.** They are all in—mentally and physically. They do the time. They are patient and persevering. They recognize that no pro ever got into the Hall of Fame overnight. Add up the hours that even the youngest draft picks have invested in their game and you'll see that it still took a lifetime to get where they are.

- **THEY SCOUT FOR TALENT IN THEMSELVES AND IN OTHER PEOPLE.** They want to be the best they can be and they want to be surrounded and supported by others of the same caliber. Whenever they can, they lend a hand to bring others up to their level.

- **THEY TRAIN TO SUCCEED.** They are always looking for ways to improve their and the team's abilities and overall performance. They expect everyone, especially themselves, to be motivated enough to come to the team in peak condition, but they also understand that you have to up your game all the time to remain challenged and to continue to be an asset to the team.

• **THEY PASS THE BALL TO OTHERS.** They are confident enough to give their teammates a chance to shine on the field too. They know that everyone in a championship organization gets their own ring—there is plenty of reward and recognition to go around.

• **THEY COMPETE WITH THEIR OPPONENTS, NOT THEIR FELLOW TEAMMATES.** More important, they compete against themselves in an effort to constantly top their own last or best achievements. They don't resent others' success; they are inspired by it.

• **THEY ACCEPT RESPONSIBILITY.** They don't whine about the playing conditions, make excuses for lackluster performances, blame their failures on others, or wallow over their losses. They review the tapes, see what went wrong, determine how not to let the same thing happen again, and get their head into the next game as quickly as possible. There are no postgame pity parties.

• **THEY ARE ADAPTABLE.** They prepare themselves and the team to play on all types of fields, in all types of venues, and in all kinds of weather. Even if they stumble and fall they pick themselves up and try again, changing tactics or directions if necessary. They recognize that they could get traded, but they don't let that distract them from doing the job they were hired to do the best they can. And if they do become a free agent, they find a team that needs their skills, they bring their A game to that new town, and they don't look back as if their glory days are only the ones behind them.

- **THEY TAKE CHEERS AND JEERS IN STRIDE.** They know enough to only listen to constructive criticism and praise. They also don't get cocky after a win. They celebrate, but they never forget to resume the hard work it takes to win again. And they don't let naysayers mess with their heads.

- **THEY KNOW WHEN TO BE A COACH TO OTHERS AND WHEN TO SEEK A COACH FOR THEMSELVES.** While they are good at helping their team members, they know when they need the advice of others who are more experienced than they are and they don't let pride stand in the way of asking them for their guidance.

While this whole chapter reads like a page from my dad's playbook, there is one more thing he would probably add for those of you whose place in the world is to be a team leader. Although my father was a tough man and had extremely high standards, he was always compassionate toward those he led. He taught me to formulate my thoughts carefully before speaking, especially before criticizing others. He urged me to consider what else might be going on in a person's life or what might have happened on that day, especially if the person is typically a solid player. *He wasn't suggesting that I withhold criticism; he was advising me to deliver it in a way that guaranteed it would be heard and understood, or to wait for another day when clearer heads prevailed.* We are all passionate people in my family, so we were not above raising our voices when we wanted to emphasize a point, but generally we thought about how we might receive criticism ourselves and used that as a starting point for the tone of our conversations. My dad reminded me that just because we're all adults, or because our driver's license says we're a certain age, doesn't mean we all receive or process information the same way. Because hearing criticism makes many people feel vulnerable, he urged me to treat them with the same sensitivity I'd extend to a child. He didn't mean that in a condescending way, but rather in an infinitely respectful way. He simply wanted to ensure that people would hear what I had to say without feeling defensive. He emphasized that the point of sharing criticism with people is to make them better, not to diminish them.

He also taught me to pay close attention to each of the people on my team—to pick up on their energy, their affect, their demeanor. To question why they might not be smiling as much as usual. He would remind me that everyone has value, a life outside of work, a story, and the same kinds of worries as I do. He'd emphasize the importance of using what I observed when talking to them. *He knew that for your case to be heard you first have to know who you are talking to and what kinds of issues resonate with them.* For instance, you might deliver a motivational message somewhat differently to a person who is single than you might to someone who is married with children, but the underlying message would still be the same. He tried to impress upon me that because two people have different day-to-day experiences doesn't mean that they have different values. To reach them both, you just might have to speak to those values in different ways. Basically, he wanted me to be sure that while I was motivating a group, I never forgot about the individual. A team is made up of component parts and they all have to do what they do best for everyone to succeed.

I genuinely hope these words about working together and being an advocate for yourself and others within a group are helpful to you in your career and in all of life. I rely on them all the time to help me communicate best with my team. And by team, I not only mean my colleagues, I also mean my family; my dear friends who lend me so much support; all the people who factor into my child's growth, from his teachers to his coaches and his caregivers—the people who comprise the core group in my life—and even those on the periphery. I mean everyone who helps make it possible for me to do the kind of demanding work that I do. They are all team players and advocates too.

CHAPTER 6

Changing Careers

One of the most frequent questions I am asked today is how I made my transition from the courtroom to the television studio. Looking back, I realize just how lightning fast that segue was for me. Fortunately, it was also seamless.

I loved my work in the San Francisco DA's office, so when Gavin's public role called for me to make a change, it was a very logical progression to go from trying cases to analyzing them. So many complex and compelling trials were making headlines at the time that my knowledge of the legal system was a positive attribute for the various news outlets I joined. My experience addressing the media after some of the bigger cases I tried, and during Gavin's political campaigns, also gave me some prior practice in front of the cameras. *While this move seemed to happen almost overnight, the truth is it was a very organic one, which I believe is at the heart of all successful transitions.* Despite the fact that I came from a different profession, the two fields I was bridging had just enough in common for me to be qualified and were just different enough to ensure that I would learn, grow, and be positively challenged in my new role too. These are, in my opinion, the best conditions under which to change fields.

But today, career change is occurring at an unprecedented rate and for a variety of complex reasons. My hope is that understanding them can help you navigate *and* advocate for yourself far more effectively.

Experts are telling us that a fair number of you readers will hold more than fifteen jobs in your lifetime and that several will be in different, albeit related, fields. Job hopping is an actual trend these days and the Bureau of Labor Statistics has the numbers to prove it. People are no longer changing jobs once every decade the way they did in my dad's day. The youngest segment of the workforce is switching jobs on average every three years.

This movement plays out in several different ways. Some people zigzag from one company or industry to the next, trading off the unique skills and perspective they bring with them for advancement. They realize they can move up in the world and in pay scale faster that way than they could if they remained at the same company and competed against people with the same frame of reference for the few in-house promotions that open up. Others are becoming gig workers—independent contractors who move freely between jobs and industries by project, applying their skills wherever and however they are needed, sometimes participating in a field for only months at a time. The diversity builds their experience and confidence and allows them to set their own earning potential.

The reasons for this type of movement are as varied as the jobs and industries themselves. For some people it is simply a matter of organic growth, as it was in my case. For many young people, it's the discovery that the field they chose—or the one that chose them after countless interviews—is no longer interesting or challenging to them. For others, it's the realization that they hit a ceiling even sooner than they expected. Still others move around because they genuinely have an interest in multiple disciplines.

Because we're able to network, scout positions, and explore the workings and requirements of vastly different fields online, we're also able to instantly see how our skills and a potential employer's needs overlap. Many great matches that might not have seemed so obvious before technology are way more apparent today.

But two of the bigger reasons have to do with money and malaise. According to a June 22, 2014, *Forbes Magazine* article, the average worker is getting a 3 percent raise, but when adjusted for inflation their actual increase is only 1 percent. When you compare that with the 10 percent to 20 percent increase employees get when they move around, you can better understand the game of musical chairs that is occurring. As the article notes, people who stay in their jobs two years or longer will likely earn 50 percent less over the lifetime of their career.

In addition to concerns over slow wage increases, employees are expressing serious dissatisfaction with management styles too. According to a recent Gallup poll, 70 percent of all workers in the U.S. market say they are "disengaged" from their jobs, with 20 percent of those admitting they are "actively disengaged." What that means is most are looking at their options and the rest are ready to act on them. The study findings assign the bulk of the rift to bosses who fail to help their employees grow. The toll on public health these relationships is causing is also becoming more and more noticeable. Chronic stress is rampant in our culture. According to the Anxiety and Depression Association of America, more than 40 million Americans over the age of eighteen battle anxiety.

Whether this overall paradigm shift is a natural evolution

in the marketplace; a response to the ways technology is changing us; a means to accommodate the swelling job force as older workers extend their working years and an influx of new, highly educated workers continue to enter it; a growing rift between management's and workers' wants and needs; or some combination of *all* these factors remains to be seen.

But whatever the cause is, the American need to shake things up in life has never been more evident. If workers are moving around so much because it's a strategy that promotes growth and fulfillment—as it appears to be in many instances—then great. These are examples of people *making their case* effectively time and time again and getting the results they want. They are examples of people advocating for themselves in new, innovative, and unprecedented ways.

If it's an outgrowth of technology and we are progressing as a species into a new age, then there is little one can do but go with the flow and apply our best case-making skills so we are poised to survive and thrive.

If the movement, however, is signaling a dysfunction in the workplace that is relationship driven, then everyone needs to stop and reevaluate. Figuring out a way to find balance is Advocating 101. Both employers and employees need to explore how and why they are failing to make their case with one another and themselves in an open, fair, and consistent manner.

Again, advocating for yourself means communicating honestly with yourself and others to meet a goal that benefits both parties.

When employees are applying for new jobs in their own or other fields they should ask themselves:

- Is the movement helping or hindering them? Do they like frequent change and newness in their life or does it cause too much stress and anxiety?

- Is it an organic move? One that fits a larger strategic plan for themselves?
- Are they only making the move for more money or are they doing it for the job challenge and satisfaction too?
- Do they understand that more money usually means more responsibility? Are they really stopping to consider what will be demanded of them in a higher paying job and whether they are prepared or willing to stretch to meet those demands?
- Are they looking to help their division and their company rise, or are they just looking to help themselves rise?
- Are they representing their worth accurately and effectively enough to their current employer? In other words, are they building their case for increased opportunities and higher wages before moving on?

Likewise, when an employer is advertising a position or granting a promotion they must stop and ask themselves some questions too:

- Are they being forthcoming about the time and energy the position will demand? In the often necessary consolidation of jobs, have they reconfigured the workload in a reasonable enough manner that the job is really doable?
- Does the function of the job still fit the needs of a changing marketplace? Because if not, they are dooming their company as well as their employee to failure.
- Does the company respect the right of their employees to replenish their energies? Working long hours

is a reality of our lives, but does vacation still mean time away from the office?

- Does the company provide an atmosphere conducive to work, meaning does the office design encourage a balance of communal activity and individual contemplation, planning, strategizing, and the successful completion of work?
- Is the company investing in the ongoing training of its employees to ensure that everyone is benefitting from the latest technologies and marketplace trends?

The times are changing, and it is just as incumbent upon an employer to make a case to the employee as to why she should come to or remain at their company. In the face of the revolving-door culture, it is a myth that all employees are replaceable. According to the Center for American Progress, this turnover costs companies almost 20 percent of a leaving employee's salary in terms of lost productivity and recruiting and training expenses. The current level of movement may be bringing new talent and ideas to some forward-thinking companies, but it is hurting the bottom line of many other businesses. Forethought on both sides and mutual respect are what will restore the missing balance.

For those of you who have asked yourself all of the above questions and have found that your reasons for moving on are still strong in your mind, looking for your new place in the world via a change of employers or even a change in careers has been well considered. You also are advocating for yourself by finding a new workplace where your skills are better valued.

Initiating change is definitely a form of advocating for yourself, especially if that change is well thought out and promotes growth and the development of new skills and understanding. It is also advocating for yourself if it removes you from a situation that stifles or suppresses you. But change without a goal in sight can sidetrack you. Advocating for yourself always starts with knowing where you want to go and what you want to accomplish once you get there.

My dad held many jobs in his career just like me, and each built upon the last so that he brought valuable experience to each new employer. When I think about how he would respond in this current climate, I believe he would cheer for the people who are zigzagging and gig working if they are doing it as a means of living a fuller, more enriching life that serves themselves and their companies well, or as a means of adapting to inevitable change. But also like me, I'm sure he'd be unhappy if this movement was occurring because of a growing rift in the workplace. Clearly, from everything you've read so far, you know that my dad taught my brother and me to play to win. *As a former military man, he strongly believed in a strategic, disciplined, determined, forward-driving approach to life, but he did NOT teach us to win at all costs.* As hard as he worked to support us, and as much as he demanded from us in our schoolwork and in extracurricular activities, he knew the value of balance. He treasured time with family and friends as much as he enjoyed contributing to society via his work. He understood that it takes both to survive, be happy, and live a purposeful life. He would never have expected us to give up either one of those vital parts of our lives for the other, especially knowing that having this balance enhances both.

When my mother died, he engaged the whole family in a project. He knew he'd have to work long hours to support us, but he also wanted to have a way to bond with us during his off hours. He bought all the supplies necessary to build a regulation-size basketball half court in our backyard and together we created the space where we would play and learn about life at the same time. It was a place where our friends and neighbors gathered. It was a place where not everyone played at the same skill level, but somehow we all cooperated and had our winning moments. It was a place where we discovered being part of a team elevates many at once, makes individuals stronger too, and is a truly satisfying way to achieve advancement. It was a place where we learned to deal with disappointment—where our losses reminded us that even championship NBA teams rarely have undefeated seasons. A place where we learned values that apply equally to work and play, livelihood and life.

I think my dad would be disheartened to see how many people who were determined to win in their careers (and did indeed succeed on many levels) actually ended up feeling as if they had lost something more vital than they had gained. People who had put in the time, energy, and effort to get a great education and a job with a very respectable title and salary only felt disconnected from the team and generally unfulfilled in life. But despite being disheartened, I think he'd encourage them to press on, to make adjustments, to pursue the right circumstances for themselves, and to make the changes necessary to restore balance and joy in their lives. He'd also encourage them to do the soul-searching necessary to make the balance stick. *I know he would invite them to rethink and redefine their definition of success to include achievements beyond those accomplished at work.* And he'd applaud employers who did the same. Balance is what allows employees to come to work recharged every day. Encouraging balance is actually one way that corporations losing people at a fast pace can advocate for themselves too. Recognizing that sometimes our clearest thinking on a subject is done when we step away from it can potentially benefit us all.

CHAPTER 7

Playing by the Rules

Obviously I believe in rules. As a prosecutor for many years, I enforced them. As a team player, I operate by them. But as an advocator, I also believe in amending them when the circumstances warrant. As you can tell by the contents of this book, I consciously write and live by a personal set of rules too. I think everyone should take time out to articulate some core values for themselves. Companies do this all the time so the entire team can be on board with their mission. This is different from setting out a list of goals. This is about defining principles that actually help guide and support your choices and actions every day for life. Before moving on from the subject of advocating for yourself in the workplace, I've picked a few rules that relate to career from my own list to share with you here. I hope they inspire you to create your own list or to at least adopt some of mine.

The first rule is to *Know Your Own Worth*. My dad knew when I was younger that I would often be more critical of myself than others would ever be of me. It was during those tough times that he would remind me of all the hidden assets I possessed. The things other people might not regularly see about me. The things that are evident in my character and behavior, but that I don't necessarily highlight because I'm not doing them for an audience. He would tell me to take inventory of these qualities as they are part of my total net worth. He'd encourage me to acknowledge them in my mind as well as in my bones because they are the things quiet confidence is born from. Being an effective advocate for yourself and others will become so much easier for you if you remember some of your own best attributes, especially in your fiercest and most intense moments of self-doubt.

Experts tell us all the time that one of the biggest obstacles to success is not only failing to recognize your hidden assets, it's failing to use them too. More often than not, anxiety over asking for a raise or for additional support on a project stems from not being sure you're worth the investment. So try something for me right now—and for yourself as well. Just think about everything you do in the course of a day. When you're done listing them in about an hour or so, you'll see that the demands placed on you just to exist—to maintain a home and family life in addition to your work life—have very likely elevated your time-management and people skills to a true art form. Busy people can pretty much juggle anything and somehow get it all done. Now add to those skills all the others you've developed pursuing hobbies and special interests. You know, the work you do for a favorite charity or in local politics, your sports training, involvement in community theater, the design course you're taking, or the blog you've started writing. I think you'll find your life description includes some form of public speaking, budgeting, negotiating, mediating, and setting and achieving goals all the time. No matter what all your prior job descriptions say, I'm confident all of these other attributes can be used in a way to help you successfully fill your current job description even better. Think about the marketing person who assumes responsibility for running the book fair at her child's school. At the end of that experience she's developed increased knowledge of purchasing and retailing too. Whenever you are advocating for something you really want, it is up to you to think about the other skills—these hidden assets sitting in your back pocket—that you can draw upon. It's also up to you to help make those more discreet qualifications known when and if they apply . . . or to add them to your daily dose of confidence as needed. *It's crucial to remember that your worth lies in the sum of all your parts—who you are and what you've learned in all areas of your life.*

My point is that there are countless ways to quantify and prove your merit to your employer or anyone else who may hold the keys to something you want and need and that some of these ways are more obvious than others. I hope the other lesson in this is that you should never hesitate to use your private time to cultivate your interests and skills because ultimately this helps you cultivate added value as an employee, all while becoming a person of greater depth and range. Whenever you are advocating for yourself—at work, at home with your family, or in other social contexts—it is important to take inventory of *every* asset in your arsenal. *No one will give you more in life than they think you are worth. And they won't know what you're worth unless you are able to tell them.*

By the way, when you really take stock of and *own* your complete net worth, you will very likely stop doing some of the things that tend to sabotage your success. Once again, ladies, I'm talking about us. We could draw up a long list of attributes—both visible and hidden—and we could present them to the world dressed like the true professionals we are and multitask brilliantly while we're at it. But if we continue to say "I'm sorry" with the frequency that so many of us do, we will sadly undermine our value before we can ever convince anyone that we have the worth we really do. So please, let's use the word sparingly—only when it is truly required. If it's just a bad habit, as so many people claim it is, then vow to break that habit or it will detract from others' assessment of your worth. Phillippa Lally, a health psychology researcher at University College London, tells us that most habits can be broken on average in just sixty-six days. If you have to, put a money jar in your office and fill it with coins every time you utter that phrase for the next sixty-six days—the way people used to do when they were trying to stop a child from saying bad words. And please make every effort to avoid instilling this habit in your daughters. When we dismiss our thoughts first, we are granting others permission to do the same. I know you don't want that for yourself, and that you especially don't want that for your children. Now let's go out there with greater self-awareness and prove our worth to the world.

One final word on knowing and expressing your worth for all you awesome women who are currently stay-at-home-moms: it used to be difficult for those of you who do unpaid work to state your value in terms other people readily understand. But now Salary.com has developed a salary calculator called the Mom Salary Wizard that you might find incredibly useful. It can help you translate the intangible contributions you make to life every day into an easily quantifiable expression. The developers of this tool have looked at all the tasks stay-at-home moms typically perform during the course of a week and they've calculated the value of these jobs on the open market. Did you know that the average stay-at-home mom works more than twice the traditional 40-hour workweek? Tallying the base pay for commensurate work done outside of the home during the standard workweek and adding in the overtime you all put in, many of you would be paid in excess of $100K per year. You know the work you do is priceless, but having that kind of information at your fingertips can certainly help you advocate for yourself in a job interview should you ever decide to return to salaried work. Check out the site. It has all kinds of valuable tools that can help you determine the salary your specific skills can command.

The next rule on my list has been slightly amended from an original rule you have all heard before. For decades so many of us have been coached to *Follow Your Passion*. I personally feel fortunate to have been raised on this principle. Because I was encouraged to do so, I identified what that passion was early in life and I pursued it with everything I had. I planned each step and worked hard to get from one point to the next. And now I'm considered expert enough to share my experience with you. I really love being an advocate, whether it's in a court of law or the newsroom, and I believe I do it well because of that passion. It would be great if everyone I knew felt that way inside. I look around me and see many others who have also pursued what they love to do, and their success is very evident. They have built pioneering businesses and have made huge differences in people's lives. They are impact players. They hardly distinguish between work and play because the two merge so seamlessly together.

But I also see a lot of people caught up in the momentum of other people's goals. They work long hours to meet the passions and expectations of their bosses, peers, and families. Sometimes they are people whose own passions may not be profitable so they choose to do something else for a living. Often they are people who just like to keep work and play separate. Or they are people who simply haven't found their passion yet. They are still searching. They could even be people whose passion is actually *being a generalist*—someone who loves to explore lots of different interests across many different fields.

Today many mental health experts and career advisers are suggesting that if you don't know what your bliss is yet, you should at least learn to love the job you're in and see where it leads. Many people have been pleasantly surprised to discover something they didn't love at first actually became a passion later as they delved deeper into it and developed more skills and knowledge. You can still lead a purposeful life doing something that you like until you find something you love. Alternatively, you can expose yourself to lots of different fields to help you find the one that stirs the heart and mind equally, as some of the job hoppers we discussed earlier are doing. We all serve different roles in moving ourselves and the world forward, and every role has value if you do it with commitment. So for those of you fortunate enough to know what your passion is, then by all means follow your bliss. For those of you still exploring, learn to approach each opportunity with an open and inquiring mind. You will emerge with skills you never knew you had, and can apply all of them to your passion if and when you discover it. You will also be truer to yourself, and that is what lies at the very core of being the best advocate you can be.

Another favorite rule of mine is *Don't Be Afraid to Take Risks.* Whether the risk is in the area of career, romance, health, or some other equally important aspect of life, I always start by examining the pieces of the opportunity that are *known* to me. The more you explore the situation by comparing it with similar experiences you've already had, the more you realize that you are not venturing into as wide a field of unchartered territory as you may have thought.

If a part of that field is still virgin territory to you after looking at it this way, then ask someone else who has taken this risk to share her experiences with you. At the very least, doing this helps you vicariously explore the *unknowns* before you make the decision to try it yourself.

Once you've narrowed the fear factor down to just a few legitimate concerns, you are ready for the next step, which is to just lay your pride aside. Look at it this way: in the scheme of life, your successes and failures are really rather small in number when compared with your efforts. When most people try something, it moves them forward or backward a little bit, but never far enough in one direction to qualify as an outright success or failure. If you don't prepare at all, you're likely to land closer to failure. Right? If you prepare a lot, you're likely to land closer to success. Make sense? What it all comes down to is this: prepare and you will minimize your risk substantially.

On the off chance that you thoroughly prepare yourself and still fail, then at least you've learned something in the process: how to do it better next time and succeed. These kinds of efforts are *incremental successes* in my mind.

In the end, risk is really based on how completely you anticipate and prepare for a situation *and* how you ultimately choose to look at the results. With pride out of the equation, hopefully you can weigh the risk more clearly. Pride is dangerous and it can be deadly if you let it get in the way.

In some situations, this may be way too much thinking. There are times when we are presented with a good situation and over-analyzing it just mucks things up. That's when you simply have to listen to your gut. Many doctors say the gut is the second brain. Our stomach churns when we're nervous; we get butterflies when we're excited; ulcers signal when we're under too much stress. In more situations than you may realize, your gut is thinking for you and will tell you whether to take the chance or not. You just have to listen to it. Those gut feelings you have are actually *instincts*. And instincts are developed by trial and error—doing something often enough to have a *feel* for it. If you have an instinct for something, it stands to reason that you have been taking small risks all along and have been refining and improving your responses to those risks by actually minimizing them. *You are more ready than you realize.* It's not too different from the way extreme sports athletes train. They usually don't just wake up one day and realize they can expertly perform death-defying feats. They usually take baby-size risks, toddler-size risks, adolescent-size risks, and adult-size risks before taking quantum, champion-size ones.

I love something Sheryl Sandberg once said. "If you're offered a seat on a rocket ship, don't ask what seat! Just get on." In those situations even listening to your second brain is too much thinking. Just go for it. Don't let fear talk you out of a serendipitous experience you've probably been training for all along.

And finally, there's a rule my dad emphasized repeatedly throughout his life: *Don't make everything about yourself.* This is especially true as you try to build your sphere of influence. For instance, it is way more effective to really *connect* with others than to just network. I have an enormous contact list—one I've actually been building since I was a little kid. I used to watch my dad methodically write down the context in which he met a person and what they talked about on the back of every business card he collected and saved. Now whenever I meet someone of interest I save his information too. I don't do this for career purposes only. I find that there are also personal advantages to meeting and staying in touch with a wide variety of people. The world is filled with so many fascinating men and women, I just think you owe it to yourself to maintain ties with those you are fortunate enough to meet as they are passing through your life. I believe there is always a reason why they were put in your path. And that reason may not always be to benefit you. You may just be the conduit between them and someone else they may be intended to meet.

This happens more than you think, especially if you revisit the list regularly enough. I check it from time to time to see if anything I've read recently or anyone else I've just met could be of interest to another person I know. I'm kind of like a human LinkedIn that way. But I don't introduce people unless I think their meeting will be mutually favorable.

Advocating for other people this way is just good karma. It's simply the right thing to do. Because I think of other people frequently, they think of me too. I can't tell you how many times someone has introduced me to a person whose expertise was useful to me at the very moment I needed it—whether it was someone who helped me access better medical care for my dad, relevant information about possible schools or sports programs for my son, real estate tips for myself or my brother, or valuable work-related opportunities. Sometimes they made the introduction simply because the other person was someone they thought I'd enjoy knowing. If done right, networking has the power to make things happen and change lives. It can really contribute to world progress as well as your own.

If you have a contact list but you're not interacting with the people on it in a meaningful and consistent way, then promise me you'll take five minutes each week for the next month or so to think about the people you've met during the prior seven days. Is there anyone on your list who could benefit from what just one of those new acquaintances does, personally or professionally? Or equally as important, is there anyone you know who can help this new person with his or her endeavors? If there are no clear-cut connections in your mind, don't worry about it. You get a pass for the week. You don't need to put two people together just for the sake of putting them together because the idea behind this practice is to make *quality* connections. Also try to recall if someone has made a good connection for you recently. If he has, don't pass up an opportunity to pay the favor back. It feels really good. If there is someone who comes to mind in any of these scenarios, send both people a quick note of introduction, adding a line or two about why you thought they might enjoy getting to know each other. Then leave the choice to connect up to them. And remember, whenever you put two people together, you should do it without expecting anything in return. *Give freely and often.*

While you are looking at that list with other people in mind, don't forget to take a moment to be kind to yourself too. Glance over it one more time to see if there is anyone you haven't been in touch with for a while whom you would like to reconnect with. Then send that person a note letting her know you are thinking of her. Casually fill her in on any new events in your life—personal or professional as is appropriate—and be sure to ask about what is happening in her life. Again, don't expect anything more to come of your note. You are simply strengthening and renewing old ties. If there is an opportunity to be had, you have just cleared the pathway for it to flow to you.

If you'd like to increase your contact list, that's easy too. You don't have to go to mixers with thousands of strangers. Just make a point to go out with a group of friends on a fairly regular basis. When you do, bring along a friend the others don't know and invite your friends to do the same next time. For instance, if you're going out with co-workers, bring along a college buddy who shares some of your colleagues' interests. When you become a facilitator like that, others will follow your example. Before you know it, you're not only helping your friends meet new people, you're meeting new people too.

Sometimes you don't even need to do anything different from what you are already doing. If you engage in activities you enjoy, just increase your awareness of the other people around you. They're likely contacts because they share the same interest too. It's easy to start a conversation with a total stranger at a gallery opening if you both love art, or to chat up the person next to you at a wine tasting if you're really into enology (or even if you're not). Building a meaningful network can start very simply with you and another person connecting over a common interest.

My mother and father always had friends of great integrity, ingenuity, and caring because they met so many of them while doing volunteer work, so that's another option to consider as well. Conversation just naturally flows when you're spending long hours doing something for someone else together.

Finally, strike up a conversation with someone you pass every day or see at the coffee shop or on the bus. She may just be a designer who can help you with your company's new branding project, a fitness trainer who can share some tips to help you get motivated to exercise again, or a portfolio manager who can make you rethink your 401K investment options. Even if you don't see an obvious connection to your world, but you still think the person is interesting, it's worth asking for their contact information. You never know when you or someone you know will need their skills. That's how networking works.

In every one of these instances you will be meeting new people who have the potential to help you and to be helped by you. As an added bonus you will be learning, growing, and becoming a much more interesting contact yourself and that to me is advocating for a better life.

My dad enjoyed meeting new people like this all the time. He thrived on it. He could talk to *anyone* because his interest was genuine. I remember watching him speak with Prince Charles and Camilla, the Duchess of Cornwall, at a state event and noticing that he was as at ease with them as he was with any of the local community organizers he met with during campaign season. While his love of people was innate, I think it can develop in all of us. Don't be afraid to put yourself out there. The reward is *great*.

PART II
ADVOCATING AT HOME

CHAPTER 8

The Power of Friendships

W hen most people think of advocacy, they think about it being exercised in public arenas. It's just easier to see how it works in a corporate setting, in a court of law, in legislative reform and public policy, and through our active volunteerism and involvement in a wide variety of charities and social causes. But whether we are aware of it or not, we also advocate for others and ourselves in more private settings and relationships every day. *Mastering this art at home is what frequently gives us the skills and confidence to do so in the larger world.*

From the time we make our very first friend to the time we date, get married, have children of our own, define our family values, send our kids off to school, and see our parents—and ultimately ourselves—through our final years, we are advocating for ourselves or someone we love. And it definitely happens every time we field one of those crazy curveballs life tends to throw at us with intense velocity and speed. *Even if you haven't reached some of these life milestones yet, preparing for them now ensures you'll be a better advocate later.* For this reason, I wanted to set aside a significant portion of this book to explore these other areas with you, starting with a type of relationship that definitely played a pivotal role in my own life and I hope in yours too: friendship.

I'm sure many of you have heard friends describe themselves as a mutual admiration society, but I really believe that a more apt description of friendship is a mutual *advocation* society. As mentioned earlier, when we are young, learning to stand up for ourselves with family is relatively easy because they understand us just by virtue of living with us. It's advocating with total strangers, especially authority figures, that's hard. *But friends tend to provide a comfortable middle ground where we can really learn to articulate and assert our needs, and respond to others' needs as well.* They start out in our lives as strangers, but if we advocate for them and ourselves well enough in the relationship, they ultimately become more like family.

When I was a prosecutor, the presence or absence of a victim's or defendant's friends in the courtroom always said a lot about them and their life circumstances. I often wondered if having better friends—or better influences as we sometimes call friends—could have kept many of them out of the trouble they found themselves in. It was easy to see how as kids, one wrong choice—or even one right choice—made at the coaxing of a friend could have changed the course of a lifetime for some of those we were prosecuting.

It was just as sad to see that sometimes I was the only one present for the victims—the one person there to step up and fight for them. Fear of reprisal might have kept some of their friends away, but if your dearest friends are not at your side in adversity, they aren't good friends at all. If you ever doubt the value of friendship and family, think about being in the most dire of circumstances without the support of someone close to you, and you will see just how important it is to have people in your life who care about you and support you.

I have fortunately been blessed with some of the most extraordinary friends. The same week I began writing this book, I was honored at an event held by an organization very near and dear to my heart. The Esophageal Cancer Education Foundation was acknowledging the work I had done as one of the foundation's board members. I'd spent the last five years helping to acquaint the public with the early signs, preventative measures, and treatments for the devastating disease that claimed my father's life and the lives of all too many others. As I looked at the dais where my good friend and Fox News anchor Jamie Colby was serving as emcee, and around the table where other close friends and family members also gathered to support me, I saw the faces of people who had been there for me when I was struggling through some really difficult times, especially through the loss of my father. They were people who stuck with me and encouraged me to find ways to triumph over that pain. And they were there that evening to celebrate the fact that I had indeed found a way to turn my loss into something positive. Bob and Rowann Villency (my son Ronan's grandparents), Shawn McSweeney, Susan Shin, Ainsley Earhardt, Andrea Tantaros, Dr. Dendy Engelman, and Dr. Kathryn Smerling are just a few of those who have rallied for me in good times and in bad. I was genuinely moved by their support and especially by the fact that they had done so much to make the evening and the event a resounding success. I knew too that friends and family who couldn't attend or who lived farther away were also there with me in spirit, including my brother, Anthony, and my girlfriend Gigi Stone Woods. Many, who lived at a distance, sent me heartfelt notes that evening and did so much in the years since my father's passing as well. I am extremely grateful for the friendships of Soraya Whelton, Hilary Newsom Callan, Lori Puccinelli, and Susan McAlarney Gerdeman too. These friends have shared both tears of sadness and joy with me. In fact, Susan gave birth to her first child, Solange, within days of my giving birth to Ronan and I am godmother to her second child, Odin. I am also lucky to count Chadd Kawai, Paul Kelly, John Shanley, and Marc Honaker as long-time supportive friends.

Strong friendships have been a consistent theme in my life. After my mother died, the acts of kindness and fellowship extended to my family were extraordinary. No one ever said, "Let me know what I can do for you"; they just thought about what their needs would be in the same situation and they provided for us out of that compassion. It was amazing how mothers of friends in the neighborhood would shuttle me off to the grocery store whenever they were doing their own shopping, knowing that I didn't have the means to get there and back by myself. It was just a given that they would lend a helping hand whenever one was needed. I also remember how one of my classmate's older sisters taught a really cool dance class I wanted to attend, but it was after school and my dad worked so I didn't have a ride. My friend, whose name is Julie Fahey, told her older sister, who taught the class, and she picked me up and drove me there. Even though she had a lot of other things to do as the instructor, she still spent time after everyone else had left, helping me make my costume for the final show since all the other girls' moms were making theirs. I still have fond memories of her and that show. I danced to a song called "It's a Love Thing" by The Whispers from their album *Imagination*. It meant so much to me to be cared for in that way.

Other friends' families, including the Thompsons and the Lombardinis, would take me on vacations. I was universally looked after by these friends, their parents, and their siblings. In the process, they were being exceptional friends to my dad too.

I even adopted grandparents. There was a woman who lived across the street from me named Alma May Jelicich, whom I called Gram. She taught me everything I know about the grace of a Southern lady. She showed me how to dress, style my hair, do my makeup, and even how to walk tall by balancing a book on my head until my posture and gait were perfect. She also helped get me ready for school dances and proms. And she let me wear a pretty little ruby and diamond ring to those events. After she passed away she left me the ring. I still have it to this day. I treasure it. You can find what you are missing in your family in the form of an amazing friend. It's why I'm a big believer in the modern family. My mother was gone and so were my grandparents, but I found a great addition to family right across the street from me. I had my own bedroom at her house and even slept over there on some school nights.

As I came to find out, Gram was hurting too because her only son had died and then she lost her husband, Steve. It was just Gram and me, and we helped each other out. She taught me how to bake the most delicious chocolate chip cookies and make tapioca pudding. Through her I discovered my love for blush and Chanel No. 5 body powder. And she taught me how to drive a car. She had this big Cadillac. I remember she'd always say, "Give it some gas." She even let me use that car for my driving test. Every Sunday we watched the 49ers football game together. Those are some of my fondest memories. She had beautiful long gray hair that she'd twist up in an elegant bun. She nearly died once, but I am thankful that my father revived her. He kept saying, "Gram, the kids need you. Show me your baby blue eyes." And she did.

I had been a tomboy up until I met her, playing every conceivable sport and running basketball games in my backyard with my friends and neighbors on the court my dad, my brother, and I built together, so Gram really helped soften the rough edges in me. I credit her with teaching me some of the more important things I later drew upon in my modeling career. With her help, the many lucrative modeling jobs I got in my twenties through Grimme and the Look Agency, and my scholarship money, I was able to pay for law school.

The examples of people's camaraderie and thoughtfulness are endless. The friends I have from childhood are definitely like family to me—extended sisters and brothers, aunts and uncles. So when I read or hear about toxic friendships, I'm sad for people who don't know what having loving friends is like. *I don't believe in spending time with people who are harmful to me emotionally, mentally, spiritually, physically, or financially.* I wish that young people, most of all, would learn to cut ties with those who make them feel bad about themselves or about the other people they love and care for. Continual, intentional, or snarky putdowns have no place in a healthy relationship.

Advocating for yourself in the context of friendship starts with choosing the right people to be part of your inner circle.

In my mind, friends should be patient, reliable, and consistent. I believe in their being steadfast so you can count on them. When they say they are going to be somewhere or do something, they follow through. They don't abandon you in social situations to be with people they perceive to be more important, and they especially don't abandon you when you are in need.

Friends should be unfailingly honest too. They should help you see yourself at times when you don't have objectivity. Although their reflections should be truthful, they should also be couched in kind, considerate, and caring language. My friend Dendy calls this a love sandwich. It's when you deliver constructive criticism in a palatable way by putting it between thoughtful statements. She practices this with friends and with her husband, Devin.

Certainly, friends should be trusted confidants. They should never betray confidences by spreading rumors, talking about you behind your back, or sharing whatever you told them in private with others. They especially shouldn't exploit you on social media, where their indiscretions can be far-reaching and permanent.

They should be fair and just advisers. They should listen to you as often, and with as much compassion, as you listen to them. They should also offer guidance they know will help a bad situation improve—not advice that only compounds your problems. And they shouldn't poison your relationships with others they perceive to be competing for your time (including the person you are dating or even your spouse).

I also believe that friends should be co-adventurers and your most ardent defenders. They should encourage you to step out of your comfort zone, to try new things that will help you grow and develop. They do not encourage you to try things that will damage your health, self-esteem, or bank account. They also have your back whenever you take those scary first steps toward meeting new challenges and goals.

Finally, friends should always make you feel like you are in good company. If you feel alone, used, sad, or anxious when you are with your friends, you are definitely in a toxic relationship and you need to get out.

Are you this type of friend to others? Are they this way with you? Friendship goes both ways. If you are being a good friend to someone who is not being a good friend to you, you have to disengage. And if you are the one not being a good friend, you need to think about why, then commit to changing your ways or commit to changing friends so your friendship is reciprocated and valued.

While many people know these rules to be true, few people know what to do when a friend isn't abiding by them. That's when common sense comes into play. Different situations may warrant different reactions. For instance, if a friend says offensive things to you or others on a regular basis to get a rise out of you or to jockey for a better position in the group, reverse peer pressure might be one way to make her aware of the problem and to get her to stop. All too often, silence makes you complicit in her bad behavior. If she is gossiping about another friend or she is being rude or disrespectful, then you and your other friends can collectively and directly let this person know that what she is saying is not okay with you. When she realizes that she can't sway others to participate in her guilty pleasures, she can either leave the group or rise to your standards. The choice is hers. In many ways, this kind of positive peer pressure advocates for her to mature and become a better person. I think you just learn to do this naturally as you get older. Your other friends don't even have to speak to you about the issue. You all just pick up on the cues and shut it down before it ever gets to be a big problem.

If a friend hurts you in some other way and it was an isolated incident, then by all means speak up. Address the situation. Let it be known that you didn't appreciate what happened and that you expect more from this person going forward. As with all forms of advocating, try to understand where she may have been coming from, and what might have caused her to behave in an otherwise uncharacteristic manner. Everyone deserves at least one pass.

If, however, you doubt the other person's judgment; if you find that she is well meaning but still gives you bad or inappropriate advice or she makes poor choices of her own, it's definitely time to unfriend this person. You know the old saying "Screw me once, shame on you. Screw me twice, shame on me." You have to take some responsibility for the situation and walk away. Don't play the victim. There is no need for histrionics or drama. Friendships are the perfect ground for discovering things about ourselves, including what we will and will not tolerate. I truly believe that it's important to accept that we all mature at different rates, we all push boundaries more or less than others, and we are all competitive to varying degrees. Just move on knowing you took a valuable lesson away from the experience. Hopefully you won't make the same mistake again. If the first step of advocating for oneself is knowing yourself better so you can be clear about your needs in a situation you wish to improve, then recognize that the friendship—while disappointing in other ways—helped you do just that. It helped you discover the kind of company you do *not* want to keep. You and this friend are already headed down different paths so just continue on your way. To disengage from the friendship, stop hanging out, texting, or calling each other. There is no need to call them out or put them on the defensive. People outgrow friendships all the time. The friendships that are keepers are with people who have proved they share your values. You may not see the results of cutting ties with fair-weather friends right away, but sometimes when people reflect on lost friendships later in life they are in a better place to recognize and deal honestly with their own contribution to the breakup. In retrospect, I realize that there were times in my life when my needs were so great—certainly after the loss of my mother and later my father, and at the time of my divorces—that the balance in some of my friendships weighed more in my favor. I might not have seen it at the time, but I certainly did when I was in a better place. In most instances, my friends remained patient and I was able to correct the imbalance, being there for them when *they* needed *me*. Interestingly enough, when two friends are going through a hard period at the same time, they can actually deepen their friendship. Helping others with their problems helps put yours in perspective and allows you to advocate for yourself and someone else simultaneously, often proving to yourself that you have a lot more inner resolve than you realize.

A special note for parents: modeling strong friendships is good for your grown children as well as your young children. There may be a time later in life when friends are all they have. If they don't know how to cultivate the right ones, they will be at a severe disadvantage. This is very likely why my dad taught me to love and value my friends. Kids witness competitive and toxic interactions between adults more often than they should. The best defense against this is to treat your own friends with respect, gentleness, and warmth.

Speaking of parents, my dad was the kind of man who was a friend to all. He believed in extending courtesy and humanity to everyone you meet—and an added dose of understanding and compassion if you sensed they were going through a difficult time. But he understood that there were different levels of friendship and that you have to set your expectations accordingly. There are people who are fun to hang out with; others whom you bond with intensely over a common goal, but little else; and those you click with on almost every level. The latter are your truest friends—people who go beyond the in vogue terms *besties* and *bffs*. People who are there for you in times of both joy and need. People you care about deeply enough to be there for in return. You could meet them anywhere and under any circumstances. They could be neighbors or coworkers, classmates or total strangers who struck up a random conversation with you that led to years of cherished talks. My dad was always open to the prospect of friendship on any of these levels because he loved people, but he had a few rules of his own. One of them was you can't expect other people to be good caretakers of your personal business if you aren't a good custodian of that business yourself. He kept the details of his private life private. Those were reserved for his family and inner circle of friends. He believed in being smart about what you put out in the world for public consumption. If you tell anyone who will listen all about your problems, fears, or even your hopes and dreams without knowing their character, what their intent and motivation is for listening, or what they will do with that personal information, the responsibility for anything bad that happens is on you. He always advised us to pick and choose our friends wisely. A friend has to earn your trust and you must earn hers. He also taught us that you cultivate great friendships by being a great friend.

Finally, my dad taught me that one sure way to advocate for yourself over time is to continue to tend to longstanding relationships. We all get busy, but we should still do what we can to ensure those connections don't just slip away. All the things in life that matter require effort, attention, and devotion. Relationships are no different. "You've got to remember to water the plants or they'll die," he often said. Knowing how rare these supportive and special friendships are should make you even more committed to nurturing them. Even though I am miles away from some of my most treasured friends, I check in often. I want them to know they are in my thoughts and that I appreciate them.

Luckily, it's so much easier to stay in touch today than it was when I was in law school or when I first moved to LA. The year I came to the East Coast was the same year Facebook was launched. Can you believe it?! It kept us all in touch no matter where in the world we settled. Now I call, FaceTime, and text my friends as well. I send them articles I think they would be interested in and whenever I hear that something new and exciting is happening in their lives, I make sure to reach out and tell them how happy I am for them. I want them to know I still think about them, that they are not forgotten. I want them to know that just as they are my frequent sounding board, champion, confidant, and voice of reason, I want to continue to be that for them.

Some are still part of my daily interactions and definitely part of big decision making too. When I bought my home in the Hamptons, I sent my friends pictures of the different design options I was contemplating for all the different rooms—including the guest room. I asked them to weigh in on their favorites because I value their opinions. I love buying fixer-uppers and they know that about me. Several of them followed my progress online. For them it was like watching HGTV—they were along for the hunt, the purchase, and the renos. And I had the comfort of knowing I wasn't making all these decisions in a vacuum. As you can see, I appreciate getting my friends' perspective and input on matters large and small, and I especially love it when the work is done and they get to share the end results with me. It's wonderful when they visit and their children play with my son. We realize that we're watching the next generation of lifelong friendships develop. This is just another way of saying that true friends always find a way to stay in touch no matter what. We do whatever it takes to remain connected because we see that it's worth the effort. Few people know you better than your childhood friends. They're uniquely aware of the events and influences that helped shape you into the person you are today. They're aware of your patterns too and know what to say to help encourage the good ones and break the bad. They understand your complexities and even know the things about you that you don't often let other people see. So when they offer advice, you can be sure it's coming from an informed place. That you've stuck with each other over time obviously means that you derive value from the relationship. I relied on one such friend while I was writing this book, Shawn McSweeney, an author herself. She and I have known each other for more than forty years. We can finish each other's sentences, and as she read this book in manuscript form there were several times when she finished mine in print.

I think it's very important to know that despite all the changes life brings—new jobs, new homes, new cities— you can still keep a core group of people close to heart who give you emotional and psychological stability. Maintaining good counsel like that is definitely a form of advocating for yourself. Who wouldn't want motivational partners like that around? When members of your family move or pass away, it's reassuring to know you have such a tight-knit group of friends you can count on and trust—a group of friends who are now your family too.

There is another kind of friend that warrants mentioning: the work friend. Somehow that title doesn't do the relationship justice, but it at least reflects the daily interaction you have with this person and the shared common interests and experiences that lie at the heart of the friendship. People ask me all the time what the work environment at Fox is like, and I must tell you it is a great place for meeting people you admire and can relate to. I already spoke about how special Dana Perino, Eric Bolling, Andrea Tantaros, Greg Gutfeld, Bob Beckel, and Juan Williams are to me. And about the kind of wonderful camaraderie I enjoy with Bill O'Reilly and Sean Hannity. But there are many others who have become treasured friends too.

I count Ainsley Earhardt among the best of them. She and I met when I first arrived at Fox. She is the type of person who feels like warm morning sunshine on your face. I can't be in the same room with her and not have a good time. She has been a loyal and steadfast friend from the start—she's consistently been there for me through many life changes. I absolutely adore her. I love her company, I love her warmth, and I love her caring nature. What you see on television is what you get in person with Ainsley. That's her true personality. If she shows up at your house for dinner she'll always come with a hostess gift—a great bottle of wine or a basket of goodies wrapped perfectly and topped with a Lilly Pulitzer bow. She exudes kindness and Southern charm. She is beautiful inside and out. I'm very, very proud of her. It's so wonderful to see her on *Fox & Friends First*.

Harris Faulkner is another dear friend. She's the type of person who takes care of everything and everyone. I love that she just announced one day that she was going to help me redecorate my office. Although I am always excited to come to work, Harris knew I had gone through a lot in my personal life since arriving at the network and the memories of those events were still fresh in my mind. She thought I could use a new start, so she helped put me on a path to one. I was hesitant at first to embrace change and to take on another project, but now my office looks unbelievable. Not only is it warm, bright, and inviting, everything in it was selected to reflect my personality. It makes me feel so good to be there and everyone who comes in compliments it. I promise you, when Harris Faulkner puts her mind to something, it's happening. She was so cute. She would come in, saying, "Okay, we're going to put an accent color on the wall here, and a mirror there." She even picked out the carpet and bought amazing furniture. I was cracking up. She took charge of the whole thing and even managed to do what no man has ever been able to—get my credit card! She's *that* good. Now when I enter my office I only think of happy times. It just goes to show you how something like that can give you a whole new perspective. It can change your focus, your energy, and your emotions. Fox isn't just the place where I work. It's become part of my life, and great women like Harris help complete that life. They are a big part of my story.

Bear in mind that Harris is a woman with two children, a husband, a television show, and countless other projects to attend to, but she still made time to help me. And speaking of her family, every year she sends out a Christmas card with pictures of her husband, Tony, and her daughters, Bella and Danika. The card recounts the wonderful things they've done together as a family and a team throughout the year. I always keep that card on my desk for at least six months after Christmas because in many ways it's what I strive for. Those cards hold the promise of the great family adventures I have ahead of me too.

I love Sandra Smith as well. I refer to her as Sporty Spice because, like me, she comes from a solid sports background. It's as if I'm hanging with one of the guys when we're together. She's wickedly smart. I never get tired of looking at her—she's stunning inside and out. And I never get tired of listening to what she has to say. She also has managed to balance her work with a great husband and a little boy and little girl at home. She's really cool and kicks ass. She always brings her A game and she's top notch on business. She and I are both fierce competitors, so whenever we're on *Outnumbered* together you know that it's game on. There's not a day that either one of us is ever going to mail it in. I love having a friend who drives me to be my best.

I've also enjoyed becoming fast friends with Kennedy. She makes me laugh until my sides split. She's smart, she's funny, she's irreverent, and she's an amazing addition to the Fox News Channel and the Fox Business Network, where she just launched a new show called *Kennedy.* I admire her strength and perseverance. Her whole family is still living in Los Angeles while she commutes back and forth, taking the necessary steps to relocate them comfortably to the East Coast. They are working together as a team to help her begin this next chapter of her career and life and to make all their dreams come true. She's been courageous and it's paying off. I did the same thing when I left Los Angeles, so I feel like we are kindred spirits in this way. I know this new friendship will grow stronger in the years to come and I'm really excited about it.

Elisabeth Hasselbeck is another wonderful addition to my circle of friends, just as she has been a fabulous addition to the *Fox & Friends* family after her years on *The View.* She is beloved by her peers as well as by viewers. She's always brimming with new ideas and positive energy. She has also been a marvelous advocate for those suffering from gluten sensitivities and celiac disease. Shortly after starting chemo my dad was diagnosed with this autoimmune disorder, so I know how challenging it can be to manage. Her bestselling books, *The G-Free Diet: A Gluten-Free Survival Guide* and *Deliciously G-Free: Food So Flavorful They'll Never Believe It's Gluten-Free*, have brought solutions to many people's daily lives. Her gift for balancing work, family, and lots of other special interests, including writing, is inspiring. Bob Beckel and I were very happy to cohost FNC's 2014 New Year's Eve special with her and Bill Hemmer. It was a great way to ring in the year. She is a true pleasure to be around and to work with.

I'm incredibly fortunate to have become friends with Megyn Kelly too. She has always been so supportive and warm toward me. She used to have me on *America Live* as a regular. I'd appear on her hugely popular segment, "Kelly's Court." I just love watching her do her thing. She is unbelievably talented—a force to be reckoned with. She has such a fierce tenacity. She pursues a story with a line of questioning that rivals some of the greatest trial lawyers I have ever worked with. Megyn represents the future of news. She doesn't take a partisan approach. She just wants to get down to the bones of the story. Even the *New York Times* has seized on this, citing her ability to create a "Megyn moment." She's respected because she'll take on the tough stories and ask the tough questions no matter where they lead. She's so dogged and intense; you can't stop watching her. I would put her up against any guy any day and good luck to the guy. Somehow through all of this, she's also managed to find the keys to the kingdom, achieving that perfect harmony between work and home life. I admire her relationship with her husband, author Doug Brunt, and their three children, Yates, Yardley, and Thatcher.

And I am especially grateful for my friendship with Greta Van Susteren—a woman I've admired for many years. She set the journalistic standard I try to live up to every day I'm on the air. I first became friends with her when I was trying the dog mauling case against Noel and Knoller. I was so excited every time she called to ask me questions about it. I loved when her number flashed on my pager. It made me feel like I was big time. I used to love to watch her show *Burden of Proof* with Roger Cossack when I was a prosecutor. It was must-see viewing for me. I really respect her work, her passion for the news and for law, and her determination to get the story out there. She has been incredibly supportive of me since the first day I walked in the door at the Fox News Channel. She is both a role model and a mentor, and the hardest-working woman in television. She has a unique brand of journalism. She forged the way for women in cable with her in-depth analysis of high-profile cases including the 1994–95 O. J Simpson criminal trial and later the Natalee Holloway case, as well as such civil trials as the Elian Gonzalez custody battle. She also played an integral role in covering the voter recount in *Bush v. Gore* after the 2000 presidential election for which she earned the American Bar Association Presidential Award for Excellence in Journalism. She is widely admired and respected and for very good reason. She has interviewed U.S. presidents, notable cabinet members, U.S. senators, members of Congress, governors, as well as numerous other world and spiritual leaders. She also traveled with First Lady Laura Bush on her tour of the Middle East to raise awareness for breast cancer. She was recently named one of the World's 100 Most Powerful Women by *Forbes* magazine. I enjoy being around her keen mind and great energy and am incredibly inspired by the work she and her husband, John Coale, are doing for the people of Haiti. Their tireless advocacy in the wake of the horrific earthquake of 2010 helped to save thousands of lives. In particular, her one-hour television special brought the plight of cholera victims there to the world's attention. The Greta Home and Academy, founded by Samaritan's Purse, was named in her honor. Located in Léogâne, the epicenter of the earthquake, this home now provides a safe haven and education for vulnerable and orphaned children.

Even before coming to Fox I met one of my longstanding friends, Gigi Stone Woods, when I worked at ABC News. We affectionately call each other sisters to this day. She introduced me to my former husband Eric, so in many ways she is responsible for the biggest blessing in my life today—my son, Ronan. Many other wonderful friendships were born at work in some way too. One of my dearest friends, Sharan Johal, and I attended law school together and then later worked on opposite sides of the legal system—I'd put people away and she'd set people free—but we still bonded over our love of the law. She also lost her father and used to call my father Dad. She was at our side in the hospital every step of the way. Similarly, my wonderful friend Wendy Segall and I became friends when I took over her cases in the LA DA's office and I loved the way she kept her files. I absolutely had to know who this person was! We have such similar minds and styles. And I also met Susan Shin and Kathryn Smerling through work associations. Susan, an intellectual property lawyer, brand marketing expert, and PR guru, is everything a best friend could ever be—loyal, generous, supportive, and she has a great mind too. We love keeping up with each other's rapid-fire pace. And Kathryn, who is a psychologist of record with the Department of OBGYN at Mount Sinai Hospital and on the Deans Council of the NYU Silver School of Social Work, as well as a frequent guest of *The Willis Report* on FBN, is valued for her wise counsel on matters of all kinds.

I suppose the moral of these stories about friendship is that if you shop around for a great place to work, you will very likely find a treasure trove of wonderful friends there too—friends you have many things in common with.

CHAPTER 9

Dating and Marriage

As much of an emotional roller-coaster ride as they can sometimes be, early romances provide some of the best advocacy training you are ever likely to receive. Most people discover how to take risks, reveal more of themselves to others, voice constructive criticism, and assert their own will during their dating years. They learn *when* to say yes and *how* to say no. And even when a relationship ends, if they are honest with themselves, they can begin to reflect upon and improve who they are and how they interact with others.

The tricky thing about these relationships, however, is that they often defy the first rule of advocacy, which is to know what it is you want before you pursue it. For many people, dating is actually the process that helps them discover what it is they want and value in a partner and in life. They go out with lots of different people precisely to have a variety of experiences because they're *not* sure what they want yet. We all know people who approach dating like shopping at a sample sale. They try countless different designer styles to see how they feel in them. They become enamored with the playfulness of one, the edginess of another, and the luxury of a third before finding the unique combination that suits them best—the one that essentially becomes their signature style. The one that best complements them for the long term.

Somehow I did not go the sample sale route in college or law school. I'm an intense person who gives 110 percent to everything I do. In other words, I fully commit. And that's exactly what I did then. While my friends were enjoying dating someone new all the time, I completely skipped that phase and instead had very serious, dedicated relationships that ultimately led to marriage.

I wed twice—the first time, as you know, was to Gavin Newsom, currently the lieutenant governor of California, and the second time to Eric Villency, CEO of Villency Design Group and founder of the Villency Emerging Fashion Fund. I learned a lot about myself in those marriages, and even though they both ended in divorce, I hold both of my ex-husbands in high regard to this day. Each had a different list of attributes that attracted me to him. Many of those qualities would top any woman's list of wants. Smart, poised, creative, industrious, and loving are just some of the adjectives that apply. Okay, they're both handsome too! I could not have asked for a better father to our son than Eric Villency. Eric is a terrific dad and coparent, which leads me to something Marilyn Monroe so famously said, and a lesson I learned when life gave me a second chance at love and a beautiful child too: "Sometimes good things fall apart so better things can fall together."

The point of mentioning my marriages here is to note that they occurred at stages in our lives when each of us was still evolving and growing. Sure, we evolve and grow throughout all of our life, but when we're in our youth we do it by leaps and bounds.

Every new experience and success we have during that pivotal time shapes us in significant ways. Sometimes those of us who commit early don't always grow in the same directions at the same times as our loved ones. In keeping with the above analogy, occasionally we emerge from these growth spurts realizing that things don't fit quite the way they used to. Is it any wonder that people are marrying later in life than they did a decade ago and certainly later than they did in the 1950s and '60s? The average marrying age for women today is twenty-seven years old and for men it is twenty-nine. In 1990 it was twenty-three and twenty-six, respectively, and fifty years ago it was as young as twenty and twenty-two. What those statistics suggest is that it takes time to grow into our mature selves, and it doesn't always happen at the same pace as that of the person alongside you.

In retrospect, I think there is something to be said for taking your time and allowing yourself to evolve more fully. I think most people's parents have it right when they encourage their kids to slow down. Our twenties are still our formative years. "Expanding the wardrobe," or, as I say now, "diversifying the portfolio" is not a bad idea. Different people stir different emotions, interests, and responses in you, so dating different people can provide the benefit of getting to know yourself better while you are getting to know them.

Don't get me wrong, I am happy my journey has taken me where it has. I have many blessings in my life because of that journey. And I know there are still more blessings to come. I believe in love. In fact, I believe in *GREAT* love. No matter how many times I fall I will always get back up and try again. I think it's worth it to put yourself out there. I think it's worth it to take the chance. And I think it's worth it to learn from your past.

As I've reentered the dating world I find I'm wiser than I was before. I certainly don't have all the answers, but my soul-searching, observations, and experience have afforded me greater insight.

What I've learned is that for marriages to last you need to remain on a parallel path—growing and progressing at roughly the same pace, or at least trading off and giving yourself or the other party a chance to catch up at all times. For that to happen you need to know yourself, your partner, and the path really well. As you meet different people and as you begin to feel more deeply toward one than the others, there are a number of things you should think about and discuss with each other to help guide you both toward a more successful union.

The first has to do with shared interests. When you first start dating, it always feels as if you can't see enough of each other, right? Even after going out for a while you may make compromises about what you'd like to do, occasionally caving in and doing what the other person prefers because you want to spend more time together. It's all very exciting. But for the long haul it's important to make sure you have enough in common to enjoy your time together and that you have enough time apart to explore the things that make you uniquely you. In general, is one of you more of a homebody while the other is more of a socialite? When dining out, does one of you consistently enjoy going to high-end restaurants while the other enjoys eating at local dives? Does one of you prefer active pursuits in the great outdoors while the other loves nothing more than attending a lecture or seeing the latest exhibit at an art museum? As life gets busy with family and other obligations, days off become more of a valuable commodity than ever. If you both have different ideas of what recharges your batteries, you might find it challenging to relax in the ways that you need to and still have as much fun together as you'd like.

Another important thing to do is engage in a little baby talk. No, I don't mean cooing and bestowing adorable pet names on each other, though that's cool too. What I mean is ask the quintessential premarriage questions *Would you like to have children someday? If so, how many? And how far down the road?* These three questions have become increasingly important as couples postpone having babies until their careers are more fully launched. This later start time can affect family planning greatly, so it makes sense to know if this goal is in line with all your other shared goals—and with your body clock.

But these are not the only questions to contemplate. You might also want to talk about where you'd like to raise your children. If you live in a city far from your folks, do you think you might want to live and raise your kids closer to one of your families' hometowns? While you and your significant other may be living the power-couple lifestyle in a big city or enjoying a very nomadic existence filled with adventurous travel right now, having children sometimes makes people feel nostalgic for the type of childhood they had, and that can result in a move to a much different locale. Are you up for that future possibility? These latter questions may not be as pivotal as the first three, but they do deepen your understanding of your and your partner's desires on the subject and that is always a good thing.

Another topic up for discussion is the subject of being faithful. While fidelity is an important issue to broach, I'm really talking about your views on God. Every couple should probably ask each other *What about religion?* even if you don't think it's important to you on a very conscious or day-to-day level. Although the person you've fallen in love with may have wonderful values and is a totally stand-up individual in every way, people with different religious traditions often feel at odds when deciding how to spiritually raise their children, how to celebrate holidays, and how to cope with life's inevitable stresses. In past generations, interfaith marriage was a hot-button issue for many couples, but over time there have been enough wonderful examples of its working well that, in many circumstances, it is less of an obstacle than it used to be. My guess is that it worked well for those pioneering couples because they had to make the case to their families before marrying, and in the process, the concerning issues were resolved. So it seems wise to follow their lead and talk the subject out with each other before it becomes a challenge. These examples of success are proof that this game of twenty questions can work. These talks can do more than highlight irreconcilable differences; they can enable couples with surmountable differences to forge a path both can live with happily. Unfortunately, a long-term relationship I had in college fell apart over a difference in religion. It shouldn't be a divisive issue, but for some people it is. For other couples, however, it is a tie that binds. I know that Ainsley Earhardt and her husband, Will Proctor, have a spiritual bond like this. They attend church and couples bible study together and frequently volunteer at a soup kitchen. They get a profound joy from engaging in spiritual devotions together.

For those of you who happen to share the same religion, please don't assume that you will choose to practice the same way. Talk about how frequently you will attend services and whether you expect the other person to attend with you or if you are fine going on your own. Determine what you both want for your future children.

If you are of different faiths, decide which of the two traditions will become your child's. Or devise a plan to include both religions in your child's upbringing. If your partner is agnostic or atheist and you are not, the situation may be more challenging, though not impossible. It would help to decide in advance how you will talk to your children about your differing beliefs.

If you come to some agreement on the subject of religion, be very specific about how these options will work. Merging practices can sound great in theory, but can be difficult to fulfill over time without a plan. Whatever your decisions, remember to never disparage the other's views, especially in front of your children. Also, know that if you are entering your marriage thinking that your partner will change once he sees how wonderful your traditions can be, you are both apt to experience disappointment. It's very unlikely that you'll change your partner's beliefs on any of these topics and that shouldn't be the point of the conversation. When you disagree, you need to decide together if you can find some common ground or if you are too far apart on the issue.

I know in my own case, any future husband is going to have to hear me say, "Dear Jesus, help me" more often than not. My son laughs and says, "Oh Mom, you sure ask Jesus for a lot of help," because I do. I always tell him, "Oh buddy, you're right. Poor Jesus is probably very tired of hearing from me every day." We always laugh about that. But religion is important to me personally and I want the right person to respect that about me. I may not be able to get to church as often as I'd like, but boy my heart is there—my spirituality and my center are there. I pray every day. I always take a moment of stillness, reflection, and faith before I go to bed at night. It quiets and centers me. It ends the day in the right mind frame and it refreshes me for what tomorrow will bring. Faith has really been a guiding force in my life, helping me cope with all that I have gone through, and the right person will acknowledge that and be grateful with me.

I'd also add the subject of Left or Right to the list of talking points. While some people convert to a new religion in the name of love, it's not as likely that they will convert to a different political ideology for the same reason. Because politics often fall along gender lines, some couples can find themselves differing so widely on social and political issues that topics of huge importance to their lives end up being off-limits for discussion. This is especially true in times of major social change or during an election year. As the Left and Right become more polarized, it's harder and harder to skirt some issues. Your spouse is someone you are going to be making major life decisions with for a very long time. You don't only need to know where he stands on issues, but how passionate he is about them. Some couples can disagree but still keep perspective. Others are adamant that their partner be aligned with them on all issues. Take the time to figure out which category you fall into. If you accept that not all couples agree on everything, then pick the issues that are most important to you and discuss those issues openly and honestly. When you do broach these topics, pay attention to whether your partner's answers make your blood boil or whether you both end up laughing at how opinionated you can be. When you disagree, do you at least listen to each other's perspective and show respect for the right of the other to hold his own views? Or do you feel dismissed or belittled? Some couples think it's not the viewpoints that matter but how you handle the expression of those viewpoints. They recognize that their spouse's vote will probably cancel out their own at the polls, but it would do that whether they were married or not so why make it an issue at home. Others decide that life is difficult enough without adding another level of possible tension. Not everyone is like James Carville and Mary Matalin, who hold strong opposing viewpoints, but clearly respect *and* appreciate the right of the other to think individually. With all of these subjects, think about where you meet and where you diverge, talk about it, mull it over together, and decide if being on the same page the majority of the time is one of your priorities or not. Some people thrive on a good political debate. Are you one of those people?

These days, some experts even suggest you get kids smart,

meaning that just as it's important to know where your significant other stands on the subject of religion, it's important to know
where he stands on education. Is he cool with you continuing
yours, even if it means you'll be a single-income household for a
while? *And how does he feel about the quality of your future kids'
education?* Where your children attend school can affect their
long-term prospects. It can impact how they are socialized as well
as educated. School is where many children's values will be reinforced. It is also important because some of these options involve
an additional financial commitment. So just jump in and talk
about where you hope to send your children someday. Will it be a
public, charter, private, or parochial school? Or will you consider
homeschooling? At the very least, your partner will share some
of the best and worst stories from his or her childhood education
with you and you can laugh at how you both survived it all.

Another issue to be discussed is the division of labor in a long-
term relationship or marriage. This is an especially important
advocacy issue for women. I know all too many ladies who hold
the equivalent of two or three full-time jobs: their career work, a
disproportionate amount of the housework at home, and a disproportionate amount of childcare if they have kids. I also see
women who have huge financial responsibilities at work abdicate
the care of their finances to their spouses. As far as we have come,
there are still gender assumptions made about who will do what
once a couple sets up a home together. Avoid the pitfalls now by
actively observing how your partner juggles his own chores and
responsibilities. Does he let them slide? Does he frequently ask
other people to do personal things for him, i.e. an assistant, sibling, friend, parent, or *you*? What kind of example has his parents
set for him? How much responsibility was your partner expected
to assume when he was young? Did he have chores or part-time
jobs? Did he do them or somehow manage to pawn them off on

someone else? Even if you don't ask these questions, be sure to observe, observe, observe! Then talk about how you might divvy things up more fairly. Ladies, don't be afraid to delegate in the dating phase. And watch yourself too—do you insist on doing things for your partner because you fear he won't do it to your liking? If so, recognize that you are perpetuating the problem. Balance and mutual respect is the key to a successful marriage. Demand both. If you deal with this issue up front you will avoid a lot of built-up resentment and finger-pointing down the road.

It's true that no one has a crystal ball. Circumstances and people, as I said before, often change. But if you are more in sync on these issues than not, it's my hope that discussing them can actually be great fun and can engage you both in building a bright vision of your future together. I also think it can hone your communication skills because without the ability to talk with each other about the important things in life, no union can survive the odds.

There are two other talks that are necessary, both of which require a bit more finesse than the others.

The first is the sex talk. Not the one you had with your parents as a preteen, but the one that helps adults ensure their bedroom remains a happy place. Chemistry accounts for so much in those initial stages of a relationship that it's almost hard to imagine life interfering with it. But as life gets busy, couples sometimes end up having to juggle their schedules to make time for intimacy. That's why experts suggest you pop the questions, *How many times a week is fulfilling for you under the best of circumstances?* and *How many times is okay when life gets hectic, as it's bound to get?* Yes, you will want to please your partner, but if you differ widely on the subject of how often, it's a sign that meeting each other's needs may become challenging over time. Helping you figure out your long-term compatibility is precisely why you are having this conversation, so don't shy away from truly understanding your partner's expectations. While on the subject, be sure to discuss the things you most enjoy about your sex life now and let your partner know what you wish to do more of going forward. Granted, the idea of talking about this is awkward, but this is the person you're contemplating being intimate with for the rest of your life. You should be able to have this conversation. If your discomfort prevents you from doing so, that in itself is a red flag. Tell each other about your fantasies and decide together what you can do to keep sexual satisfaction and romance alive in your relationship over time. Talking about this potential challenge when it is still a hypothetical situation and not an emotionally charged one should help. Recognize throughout all of these conversations that love is give-and-take. Really listen to what your partner is saying and ask yourself if you can meet his needs without compromising your own. If both of you answer yes, you are well on your way to making your case for commitment. And the bonus is that all this pillow talk can be quite sexy in itself.

The other talk, of course, is about the sticky topic of money. The question of how couples can bank on future happiness is obviously a biggie. The next chapter is devoted to the most effective ways you can deal with money on your own and together, but for now know that, at the very least, you will need to agree on how any debt will be handled and how earnings will be divided, spent, or saved. You will also have to be frank about what you spend your money on, and what day-to-day purchases are important to you, as well as what long-term purchases you hope to make. Don't hold back. If that weekly mani pedi is crucial, put it on the list. No hiding regular, ongoing expenses from each other even if you suspect the other person will think it's frivolous. The honesty in your relationship is in the details, not just the big stuff. And speaking of the big stuff, be sure to let your partner know if you have ever filed for bankruptcy, defaulted on a loan, or if you have an outstanding or long-term financial obligation of any kind. But more on all of this later.

Because my dad had been so happily married to my mom, I can't help but think about what else he'd add to the list of considerations. I know for sure he'd gently remind you that conflicts are bound to arise no matter how many of these important issues you discuss in advance. He'd also advise you to talk about any unanticipated differences that surface later, just the way you tackled the above conversations—clearly, calmly, and respectfully.

Couples in my dad and mom's day used to say never go to sleep angry with each other and that is a good rule, but it supposes that all issues can be hashed out and put to bed amicably in a single evening. He'd probably think the better way to approach the issue is to agree to disagree until you can resume the important discussion with a clear head the next day. He did not believe in forcing solutions or tucking problems away neatly where they'd remain hidden but still active. Most likely, he'd also suggest that you look to your own history of communication and your partner's for clues as to how discussions will unfold in your marriage. Do one or both of you come from a family of yellers or verbal sparring partners? This learned behavior is bound to come out in your relationship, if it hasn't already. If a conscious effort to curb that behavior is not made, he'd tell you that it's apt to become a problem. Then he'd remind you of the elements of any constructive discussion: state your view clearly, support it with evidence, listen to the opposing viewpoint—*I mean really listen*—then either counter their argument respectfully or put forth a solution, maybe even one that entails both parties compromising. This much I'm sure of: just as he'd tell you to be quick to talk things over, he'd tell you to be slow to anger because he knew that at the core of every argument is a need to be heard. Sometimes when people argue, it has nothing at all to do with the problem at hand. *Most people will work out their differences if they truly believe their opinion is being valued.*

I think he'd also tell you that no matter how good you get at making your case, you can't have a meaningful relationship and still win every battle, so pick and choose the battles that are most important to you.

Another pearl of wisdom he'd share involves regularly scheduling a date night with your spouse. He even told me to budget the money so I didn't fall out of the habit. That date night is time for you to have a quiet conversation, to look each other in the eyes, and reconnect, away from the distraction of kids, pets, work, and other responsibilities. I've asked couples who have been together for as many as forty or fifty years and they all say this is indeed one of the secrets to their success. The other is that they take regular vacations together. Those trips allow them to recharge as individuals and as a couple, and they also create many happy memories together.

Finally, my dad would tell women to stop obsessing with one another about the men in their lives. Other women are not the best sources of that kind of relationship advice. Whenever I would chat nonstop with my girlfriends about guys, he'd say, "You're wasting your time. All the two of you are doing is going back and forth trying to figure guys out and neither one of you knows how men think." I'd laugh out loud because what he said was true and very charming when delivered in his Irish brogue and with that classic twinkle in his eyes. When you think about it, he made a good point. You really cannot get good advice from your girlfriends about men and the way they operate when neither of you is a man. You're going to the wrong well for water. I was fortunate to have my father in my corner, giving me advice about guys and relationships whenever it was needed. In his absence, I often talk to my brother. If you can, turn to your father, your brother, or a trusted male friend or colleague for greater perspective and sound advice that won't scare the guys away.

In the end, couples don't have to agree about everything. Advocating for a healthy relationship is about making room for more than one opinion. However, if differing opinions consistently impede your freedom to be yourself or prevent you from fulfilling a goal you intensely value above others at the time, then advocating for *yourself* may mean moving on.

Making the decision to end a relationship is never easy, regardless of whether you are the party initiating the split or the one just coming around to accepting it as reality. But you will know it when the time comes. It's the point when you finally give yourself permission to stop pushing against the winds of change. The point when you shift direction so those winds are at your back, propelling you forward instead of stopping you in your tracks. You may have grown as much as you can as a couple, but there are other experiences left to have in order to grow more as an individual. If you look at it this way, it is my hope that you won't see it as giving up or retreating, but rather as having the courage and the faith to move toward greater self-actualization.

When you do move on, no matter how much loss you feel at the time, recognize that no one died. Failure to sustain a relationship doesn't mean you don't still carry the memories of better times, and certainly the growth you experienced in the relationship, with you as you go forward. That, in my mind, is advocating for yourself. It's all about living and learning and improving yourself for the next time around.

CHAPTER 10

Money and Relationships

When I was little, I had an account at The Lloyds of London Bank. Its fancy foreign name sounded very swanky to me, but the branch I used was conveniently located at a nearby mall. My dad would take me there every week to deposit my allowance. I would note the transaction in the ledger of my checkbook, with its shiny green cover, and feel so proud and secure that when I needed or wanted something the money would be there. I especially liked to save for our family vacations when my dad would take my brother and me to play video games in the arcade at the Vegas resort where we stayed. My brother was less conservative than me at the time because he knew our dad would give us money on those trips and because he had a million other fun things he planned to do with his allowance while, in his mind, mine was sitting in a vault collecting dust. (Of course, it was collecting interest, too.) Once we were at the arcade, Anthony would have a blast playing one game after another. Soon I'd be sharing some of my change to keep him happy because naturally I spent what my dad gave me sparingly and always had some left over. I can't help myself. The instinct to save is in my bones. I'm not kidding—many years later I used the money in that Lloyds of London account to purchase my first car. *My point is that as young kids my brother and I represented two very different sides of the same coin when it came to money. He lived for the moment and I lived for the future.* Of course, now he is more financially responsible than almost anyone else I know. Like many people, he grew up and realized that life is not one big arcade anymore.

But this example illustrates how differently we can sometimes handle personal finances. There are people who freely spend their money because enjoying life is a priority for them. It enables them to have new and different experiences all the time. By contrast, there are those who feel compelled to save because it gives them peace of mind and a sense of security. There are those who enjoy talking about money and those who are extremely private about it; those who are pragmatic and those who are emotional on the subject; and, as always, there are countless variations in between.

There are also people who believe that how you handle your money is based on *nature*, while others would argue just as strongly that this behavior is based on *nurture*. Given the fact that my brother and I were raised in the same household and were opposites then, but are much more aligned today, I'm inclined to agree with Team Nurture. However, we all still know at least one spendthrift who can't seem to change his or her nature.

I mention this because when advocating for yourself in a relationship, it's really good to know which general profile you fit and which one your partner fits. Lucky for me, both of my ex-husbands had the same spending habits as I did, which made life in that regard so much easier. I never argued with either of them over money. We always agreed about where our hard-earned dollars would go, especially when it came to big expenditures, whether it was the rent on our apartment or the down payment and mortgage on our home. Because my dad was a builder, contractor, and landlord throughout my childhood I learned a lot from his real-estate investments, which I later applied to my own investment decisions. Being well informed, in addition to being measured and thoughtful about spending, made buying even big-ticket items together a much less stressful experience. This approach took a lot of the emotion out of the equation, leaving us with the only emotion that we wanted to have after laying out lots of money—joy.

Of course, being different in nature doesn't necessarily mean you can't have a happy marriage; it just means you need to know how to negotiate those differences when you encounter them. And that's where the nurture people's ideas can help. Negotiation is always best conducted when you understand the other party's wants and needs as well as your own. If you stop and explore what shaped each of your relationships to money, then you can take a lot of the hidden emotion out of your future discussions and purchases. You can also differentiate the things that are important to you from those that might have been important to strong influencers in your life. You can determine when you are possibly reacting to something from long ago so you can make very conscious decisions that apply to your happiness, security, and well-being today. You may still be exactly the kind of money handler you were before this introspection, but you will be better able to explain your habits to your partner in a way that helps you both work around them.

In addition to having this kind of self-awareness, it helps to speak knowledgeably about the purchases you wish to make together. Do your research. Know the pros and cons of what you are buying. Big spenders may not seem like such big spenders any-more when their homework reveals that they chose an item that lasts longer and performs better than any other on the market. Even emotional decisions, like going on an extravagant vacation, may seem less emotional when you share the reasons why you want to take that vacation and you come prepared to talk about the other things you are willing to sacrifice to have that amaz-ing adventure together. Making the case in this way can make life more enjoyable for everyone—for couples who share the same perspective on money as well as those who don't.

There are lots of questions you can ask yourself and your part-ner to get at the heart of how each of you were raised to think about money. Did you enjoy lots of creature comforts when you were growing up? Did you lead a near fairy-tale existence? Or did you just get by with the basics? If you didn't have much money, were you painfully aware of that fact, or were you blissfully igno-rant of it until you were older?

Did your parents talk about money? Worry about it? Obsess over it? Were they frugal? Generous? Or even irresponsible with their money? Did they teach you about it? Or was it a taboo sub-ject, shrouded in mystery? Did they save? Invest? Give to chari-ties?

Were they conservative? Or were they bold risk takers? Did you get allowance? And if you did, at what age? Did you save it or spend it right away? When you made purchases with that money, were they impulsive or did you really contemplate them? Did you have any of the things you bought with your childhood money for a long time or did you consider your purchases disposable? When did you get your first checkbook? Pay your first bills? Hold your first job?

Dig deep into your cents/sense memory. What are some of the emotions the subject of money evokes for you? Do you feel more freedom, comfort, or power when you have money in your pocket or bank account? Are you more generous with those you love? Does it make you feel more philanthropic toward the world at large? Do you equate it with an ability to survive and thrive? Or does it signify excess and indulgence?

Does the very thought of not having it make you fearful or anxious that you might have to sacrifice, struggle, or be dependent on someone else?

Remember that even though our financial history is imprinted on us the same way honest George Washington's face is imprinted on a one-dollar bill, once we look at why we are predisposed to think about money the way we do, we can hopefully behave more logically than emotionally on the subject. And that always helps to put couples on a more even playing field.

By the way, while it's best to have these conversations before you're married, couples that have been together for years can also benefit from them. It's never too late.

TAKING THOSE FIRST FINANCIAL STEPS TOGETHER

Once you really understand each other's past, you can actually plan and advocate for a better future. A great way to begin is by creating a budget together. By the way, *together* is the operative word here. You both have to participate and remain informed. As part of this process you should:

- Look closely at what each of you earns and any other assets you have.

- Make a list of your ongoing expenses, from car and health insurance to rent or mortgage payments.
- Be sure to include any debt you are carrying.
- Add to that your present purchase priorities—the items you've both decided you want to invest in, i.e. bedroom furniture for your new home together, wardrobe items for a new job, materials or equipment for a shared hobby, a vacation together, etc.
- Also remember to set aside a little something for unexpected events.
- Then discuss your long-term desires. If you are renting your home, are you hoping to buy an apartment or house? If you own your home, are you thinking about renovating it to increase its comfort or value? Is a new car on that list? Does one of you plan to return to school so you can increase your long-term earnings potential or change fields?

If the answer to any of these questions is yes, decide how much you can put away each month to make one of those dreams a reality, and over how many months or years you'll need to save. *Even if you view these as fantasies, they are exactly the kinds of things that can help you maintain discipline and willpower.* You might be surprised how much faster you can get to your goal when you've actually thought about and planned for it. Trade off some of the items on your more immediate priority list if you think it will help you fulfill that dream sooner.

If you haven't done so already, you should also consult an accountant to be sure you are avoiding the marriage penalty and benefiting from the marriage bonus at tax time. (By the way, I love my accountant, Jay. I count him as one of my most successful relationships.)

While you are at it, see a financial planner to set up long-term investment and/or retirement accounts no matter how far away retirement seems. You should do this even if one or both of your employers offers savings plans, as there still may be more ways you can grow your money together. Advocating for yourself financially means investigating every means that can help make your life fuller and more comfortable now and in the future.

If there are other needs for your home or family that take precedence right now over investing, then at least set a date for when you will start saving for later in life, and stick to that time frame. When you do finally look at investment options, remember to diversify. It is never wise for you to put all your eggs in one basket.

As mentioned earlier, one of my favorite investments is real estate. There are homes and apartments out there in need of some tender loving care and with an interest-only loan, a little bit of a down payment, and some elbow grease you can purchase one and transform it back to its original grandeur or into a spanking brand-new version of itself. You can opt to live in it or flip it for profit. Both are smart ways to spend your money. I know because I did this with two earlier apartments and am doing it now with my Hamptons home. The nice thing for me is that it not only helped to generate money, but it also fulfilled my passion for refurbishing, decorating, and trying out new neighborhoods, cities, and styles.

Another investment option you should consider is buying a life insurance policy. Although no one ever wants to think about the prospect of losing a loved one, especially when you are enjoying some of the happiest days of your life together, I know it's a real possibility so this is not something that I recommend lightly. If you love your spouse, you won't want to risk him or her losing all that the two of you are building together in the event one of you passes. While you know you each have the ability to fend for yourself, it's nice to have that added security. It's not just a smart thing to do; it's a genuinely loving thing to do. So get on it.

The great thing about following these steps—especially budgeting—is that even if your spending is a little tight for a while, you at least have a plan in place to help you meet your obligations without second-guessing yourself over what every purchase you make is doing to your funds. That kind of doubt can sometimes make you feel more constrained than you actually are.

And when you do finally meet your goals, you can do whatever you want with what's left over. It becomes as discretionary as Anthony's and my allowance was. You can each spend money on the things you want without worrying about how it will impact the needs of anyone else in your household. Now that's empowering!

In the end, this process often helps couples discover that they had more in common than they realized. When they share the same hopes, they can begin to discipline themselves to share the same spending practices. Notice I used the word *practice*. Before you give much forethought to spending, I'd call the way you spend money habits. But as you become more proactive, your actions definitely become practices, and practices imply that you get better at doing them over time. So have patience with yourself and don't get discouraged. *When you make a strong case to yourself and to your partner for the things you want to achieve together in life, you have double the momentum working in your favor. It's only a matter of time until you make those good things happen for you.*

Set clear goals. Plan for them. Articulate them to others who can help you make them come true. Do these steps sound familiar to you? They are the same steps people who successfully advocate for what they need and want take *every* time they go to bat for themselves. Don't allow money to intimidate you. It's like walking. In time, we can all go from taking baby steps to running.

Remember too that seeking education is always a means of advocating for yourself. If there is something that is unclear to you, investigate it. For instance, a lot of people don't know the difference between debit, charge, and credit cards, even though they use them all the time. In the information age there really is no excuse for not finding out more. You'd never use a power tool without reading the instructions first, right? Financial tools are power tools too and, while they don't necessarily come with step-by-step guidelines, the information is easy enough to find in a book or online. In this case, the pros and cons of debit, credit, and charge cards can be found right here in this book:

Debit cards are generally a great way to ensure that you don't overspend. I like using them because it's like buying with cash and I get a written record of where all my money went at the end of the month. Examining each month's expenses helps me set, adjust, and stick to a more realistic budget. I also like the automatic bill payment feature, which pays recurring bills from my account so I never fall behind on such things as my phone bill or rent. That can really help you maintain outstanding credit, which is attractive to lenders when you need a home loan or you are signing a lease for a car. Trust me, your credit matters.

The challenge with debit cards, however, is that you must keep a close eye on your balance when using them so you don't get hit with overdraft charges. You should also check the protection plan on any debit cards you use. There may be limits on what they cover in the event your card is lost or stolen and purchases are made by others under your name.

Charge cards are also a good alternative. Because they require that you pay the balance at the end of the month, they help you curb excessive spending. What's nice is that they also come with bonus programs that provide deals on services you might not otherwise be able to take advantage of. Some give 5 percent cash back and rewards on travel, among other perks. As with all cards, check to be sure that the annual fee doesn't cost more than the benefits you are likely to use. Although the protection quality is generally good on charge cards, I'd also make it a point to read the protection plan on any card carefully before using it. I happen to like using American Express because they offer great purchase protection in terms of items that are lost, damaged, or stolen. This came into play for me when my Hamptons house caught on fire. I was able to get money back for items that were damaged. Securing that kind of protection is definitely advocating for your financial well-being.

Many people think you have to pay your Amex bill off right away, but another great thing about this card is that if you are a customer in good standing you can actually request what is called a pay over time plan. Of course, you would be making interest payments, but that may be your best option if you don't have enough funds to pay off your whole balance in a given month. It allows you to pay a portion of what you owe monthly until there is no balance left. You just have to have the discipline to keep to that payment schedule so the debt can be paid off as quickly as possible. Using the pay over time plan works well if you have to make an unexpected purchase of a big-ticket item, such as a new washing machine or dryer, and you don't have all the money up front. But it's not something you would use all the time.

Credit cards: I tend to avoid using these because it's too easy to postpone payment and to rack up heavy interest charges, which can virtually double the cost of an item over time if you leave the bill unpaid for too long. But when I was furnishing my new home and my monthly expenses were higher than usual, I appreciated the flexibility this kind of card afforded me—I had a line of credit *and* the time to pay for my purchases. In situations like that, I try to be frugal in other areas of my life for a time so I can pay off the balance as soon as possible. You may want to keep a credit card around for those kinds of expenses too, but remember to exercise caution.

Hopefully these distinctions and simple ideas will help you keep as much money in your pocket as possible—and prevent you from ever having to make your case to bill collectors. Since debt can really put a strain on couples, I hope they will also keep your relationship as solvent as your bank account. Failing to investigate different financial options, or to have open and honest communications on the subject of money before *or* after getting married, is not just failing to advocate for your own financial health; it's failing to advocate for the health of your marriage too.

My dad used to offer me lots of great financial advice, much of which I have included here. One thing he might add is that while many people think these conversations are only for the wealthy because they have assets worth protecting, they are actually important for *everyone*. There are few things more divisive than working hard to build your fortune together only to discover that each of you wants to spend the results of that labor differently.

Since experts say that the subject couples fight about most frequently is money, I think he would also tell you to *be careful not to let pride get in your way*. There are times when I can be very stubborn, so I heard this advice from him enough to know that it applies to heated discussions over money too. Haven't we all gotten so invested in an argument at least once in our lives that we continued to hold our ground long after the other person made some really valid and persuasive points? Pride can be very dangerous that way because it can cause us to make decisions we wouldn't make in a more balanced moment—decisions that might cost us later. During any discussion—but especially ones surrounding personal finances—it's best to engage with open ears and an open mind. Don't get so entrenched in your position that you fail to hear a different perspective. That perspective may save you from making a huge mistake. Or if you're really lucky, it may bring you some unexpected good fortune.

Lastly, I think he'd tell you that just because you and your spouse share the same goals, got off to a good start, and made some wise decisions early in your relationship, you cannot take your eyes off the ball when it comes to your finances. He was fond of saying "Fools and their money soon part," meaning that you have to be careful with your money. You've got to earn it, watch it, invest it, and respect it even as you spend it. People's circumstances can change. There may be times when you will be living large because your jobs are paying you well, your property value has risen, or your investments are yielding strong returns. But there may also be times when savings are depleted by both planned and unplanned expenses. Financial awareness, strength, and independence are advocacy skills that are necessary through-out your entire life. Keeping a watchful eye allows you to come up with contingency plans. If both of you are vigilant, you increase your chances of catching problems before they occur and of com-ing up with workable solutions in the event they do happen. But both of you also need to be vigilant in the event you ever have to go it alone. When a spouse passes away, the person remaining often talks about feeling as if they lost a limb—as if some part of them has been amputated. This is true for many reasons, but one reason is because the person who is gone oversaw some part of the survivor's life. A division of labor still exists in the majority of marriages. More often than not, men still handle the family's personal finances. In the event of loss—or as frequently happens in the event of divorce—you don't want to be the person who doesn't have a clue about your mortgage payments, your property tax, or any other pertinent detail in your financial life.

I wish you all have nothing but good fortune and long, happy marriages, but I want to also be sure you have the information at hand to advocate for yourself if the unthinkable happens. Re-member my dad's adage: if you are going to present your case at any time in your life and under any circumstances, you better be prepared.

As a general rule, you should keep important financial records and documents in one, easily accessible place. Include copies of your prior three years income tax returns. Have the deeds to all of the properties you and your spouse own. Note how they are titled (i.e. which are in your spouse's name, which are jointly held, and which are in your name). Also note the property taxes associated with each.

People who mind their money are also aware of any outstanding mortgage or home equity loans they have; they keep bank and investment account numbers handy and they track their current balances in all accounts including their various retirement accounts—pension, 401K, and IRA. And they also are aware of their consumer debt, auto or school loan balances, as well as credit card balances.

In this day and age of frequent fraud, keeping a watchful eye on your credit report is also a must. In addition to maintaining joint cards, each of you should always have your own credit card so you have an established credit score in your own name. If one of you does not, a quick way to build good credit is to apply for a credit card. Put modest purchases on it and pay off the balance in full each month. Note that I did *not* say a charge card because charge cards don't necessarily help you establish *positive* credit. They weren't really designed to keep spending in check, so they don't count toward what is called your *credit utilization score*— the number that factors most heavily toward achieving an overall positive credit rating. Charge cards are tricky because while they won't help you secure a positive credit score, they can actually contribute to a negative score if you end up getting hit with late fees for not paying the bill on time.

People who advocate for greater financial security are also familiar with all their insurance obligations, including life, health, auto, and homeowner's policy premiums. And they keep copies of all wills and trusts.

My attention to financial details may have begun with nature *or* nurture. It may have started with my keeping that little green checkbook all those years ago, running a tight ship at home, tracking the grocery money, being accountable for returning the change to my dad, working several jobs, and helping to pay for school. I'm not sure. But this much I'm certain of: it continues because I read lots of articles, watch my colleagues on Fox News and Fox Business, and learn from the people around me who are good with money. I'm also certain that you and your loved ones can become your own best financial advocates by doing these things too!

CHAPTER 11

Supporting Your Spouse

In every relationship there comes a time when you not only need to advocate for yourself but also for your partner. Sometimes you'll be called upon to do this in momentous ways, and sometimes you'll have to do it in the kind of day-to-day ways that almost seem matter of fact.

As I sat down to write this chapter, a very public occasion came to mind first. When my ex-husband Gavin Newsom ran for mayor, he was stereotyped as someone who came from a privileged background. People imagined that he had led some kind of charmed life that would prevent him from relating to the average citizen's experiences and needs. Because nothing could have been further from the truth, I spoke up for him at various fund-raisers, town meetings, and in the media in an effort to set the record straight. Of course, while I verbally described his strengths, he demonstrated his values and his dedication to the people of San Francisco in every other way, from the content of his platform to the extent of his actions. But I felt that if I offered my unique perspective, people would come to know him the way I did.

I knew the wrong assumptions came, in part, from the fact that he happened to have some very wealthy and influential friends, in particular, Ann and Gordon Getty, whom I consider to be two of the loveliest people I have ever met. Ann played a very important role in my life and was very helpful to me when I became first lady. Gavin and their son Billy had known each other since childhood. Their fathers went to St. Ignatius Prep School together and Gavin's dad, who was a state appeals court judge for seventeen years, was also one of the trust administrators for the Getty family. As a result of Judge Newsom's work for the Gettys, Gavin and Billy found themselves at many of the same functions when they were growing up and they soon became as close as brothers. But despite having wealthy friends and a father with access to a wide range of influencers, Gavin hardly enjoyed a silver-spoon upbringing. His parents divorced when he was very young. He and his sister, Hilary, then moved to Marin County to live with their mom, Tessa Menzies Newsom, who worked several jobs to support them. Just like Gavin's dad, Tessa had an incredible sense of civic responsibility, which is no doubt what made Gavin so socially minded too. It was this deeply rooted spirit of community that led her to care for foster children while raising her own two children. For much of Gavin's and Hilary's childhood, Tessa's income was stretched to meet the demands of raising a family, as well as covering the expenses of her return to college to earn a bachelor's degree. But the family's finances were just one aspect of Gavin's struggles. He has since talked openly and fervently about his challenges with dyslexia. His diagnosis predated many of the incredible tools and reading methods available to dyslexics now, so he really had to work superhard to overcome both his learning differences and the stigma attached to them. He compensated for these challenges by giving the utmost attention to his studies. He would read and reread his books constantly. He was very driven. Once he achieved a goal, he was always onto the next one. And he worked just as hard at sports too. In fact, he got into Santa Clara University on a partial baseball scholarship.

His determination to overcome the obstacles in his life was an inspiring example of self-advocacy. You can see that same fortitude in the way Gavin ultimately filled his position and legislated for change. His own struggles helped him relate better to other people's struggles. Speaking up on his behalf during his campaign proved to be very natural and easy because the facts were all there. *Sometimes, it takes the objectivity of another person to make a strong case for you, and when those occasions arise for someone you care about you better be up to the task, armed heavily with your best case-making skills.* In retrospect, I can say that everyone who stepped up to the plate for Gavin, including myself and my father, was rewarded in the end. He accomplished a range of good things for our hometown—from bringing national attention and support to the issue of gay marriage to signing a universal health care plan into law and joining the Kyoto Protocol, which has helped to reduce harmful emissions in the city's atmosphere. His Care Not Cash program, which was introduced to better address the needs of homeless people, was an innovative measure too. It was designed to prevent the cash grants that were being given to these folks from being used to buy alcohol or drugs. Instead, it redirected a percentage of those grants toward increased shelter space, better housing, and more effective counseling, among other services.

There is another case of advocacy between spouses that I must mention because I find it so inspiring. It involves my son's grandparents—Robert and Rowann Villency—who have been happily married for more than fifty years. In observing them, I've discovered two secrets that I believe contribute to a lasting relationship because they make each partner feel truly supported and understood. I'm sharing them with you because you are never too young *or* too old to apply these pearls of wisdom to your own relationship.

The first is very simple. Although the two of them are remarkably different people, they honor their differences by giving each other enough space to enjoy their individual pursuits and to grow from them. Bob is a creature of habit and an astute businessman, while Rowann is an adventure seeker and a gifted and talented artist. Because they encourage each other to partake in the things that make them feel alive and whole, the quality of the time they spend together is richer. Naturally, they have lots of common interests too. They play golf and tennis together and they love hosting family and friends, but they recognize the importance of letting each be true to themselves. I find this kind of mutual respect one of the subtlest yet most effective ways to champion a loved one. I see this relationship mirrored in that of their daughter, Cara Villency, and son-in-law, Josh Sacks, both of whom have become two of my closest friends. I adore them. *Their example reminds us that when you make a strong case for continuing to do the things that you love, and you respect the right of your partner to do the things he loves, you really are advocating for a healthy, happy, and lasting marriage.*

The second secret is a gem too. Bob has always told me that a sense of humor is one tool that never fails him in his relationship with his wife. Laughter can heal rifts, change emotions, and redirect a conversation. If he, or his wife, is too upset about something to discuss it without emotion, he'll deflect the conversation with a little joke, knowing full well that a case can always be made more effectively on another day. It clearly works because not only have the two been married for more than five decades, but as Bob will tell you, Rowann is still his best audience.

Of course, my own parents were wonderful role models in this regard as well. My dad always advised me to look for a spouse I admire and respect. Someone whose opinions I value— and someone who is not reluctant to share those opinions with me. He once told me he married my mom because he knew she would make a wonderful mother. Although I was young when my mother died, I vividly remember the way both of my parents supported each other. My mom was my dad's biggest confidant. She would listen to and encourage all of his hopes and dreams and he would, of course, do the same for her. They had an amazingly passionate relationship. I recall how she would dress so nicely, always looking sweet and pretty for herself, but also clearly for him too. She was very feminine, very sexy. She would sit on his lap and hug and kiss him. They were a very affectionate and playful couple. However, she could also be quite serious and firm. For instance, she believed that family was one of our greatest sources of strength. She was adamant that we all have enough quality time together and was very vocal about that. Family dinners were a must in my home, and on days when my dad had to work the overnight shift, it was understood that dinner would be served extra early so he could enjoy our company and a wonderful home-cooked meal before he left. My dad was never afraid of anyone, but he knew my mom was powerful when she was being driven by purpose and he didn't dare mess with that. If you don't know what I'm talking about, then you never dated or were married to a Puerto Rican woman. If there was something she thought we should be doing to improve ourselves or to benefit us all, she let us know about it. Because her thoughts were always clear, well reasoned, and rooted in love, we'd all naturally comply. She was fiercely passionate and I know my father truly respected that about her. He understood that conviction is necessary in good advocates, and he agreed with her about the value of family time. But even when they didn't see eye-to-eye on an issue I know he still appreciated hearing her side of things. You might think that being with someone who agrees with you all the time would be great, but the truth is there is no growth in that. If your core values are well matched, then thoughtful, articulate, and caring exchanges of differing points of view can actually help expand your thinking and enable you to grow individually as well as together.

CHAPTER 12

Teaching Kids to Advocate
for Themselves

When my son, Ronan, was seven years old he researched, comparatively shopped, and was ready to purchase a moto-cycle online. Boy was I glad he didn't have access to my credit card in time to push the send button. After I got over the initial shock of how savvy he had become, he gave me a rundown of his reasons for wanting it, selling me on its features better than a car dealer could sell me on a 2015 Mercedes Benz in diamond white with a soft beige leather interior. But the high-tech dirt bike he wanted was intended for twelve-year-olds so no matter how well my son prepared and made his case to me, I had to say, "No, buddy, that bike is not in your immediate future."

Just like every other child, if Ronan sees something he'd like to own (which, by the way, is a golf cart this week), he will appeal to me for it with every persuasive argument at his imaginative disposal, especially if it's something he believes is going to be the source of endless hours of fun. But as easy as kids can make it look sometimes, they don't necessarily come hardwired at birth to be able to make their case. It's not some innate ability that just kicks in by the time they're eight. It has to be molded and shaped from a very young age so they are prepared to use those skills to advocate for themselves in more difficult situations, not just for purchasing power.

Teaching your children how to be the best advocates they can be in all matters of life starts even earlier than you may think, and is, for some parents, far more difficult than they ever expected it to be. When toddlers are learning to walk and master the physical world, parents seem to intuitively know that they have to let them do some things for themselves to progress. Of course they don't let their little ones roam around without some guidance, and if they are going to let them stumble, they find a soft carpet for them to practice on first. The same is true when teaching your children to think, speak, and act for themselves. *You must model ways to do it, put them in safe spaces to experiment, and then let go and watch them take their first strides.* As difficult as it is at times, you have to resist the urge to jump in whenever they so much as teeter. Given the complexity of the world today, too many parents continue to advocate for their children well beyond an appropriate age. It's understandable, but in the long term it's very damaging because our children will be less equipped to deal with difficult situations if they never get so much as a dry run. Of course, you can intervene if the situation is beyond them or if there is present danger, but other than that you really must let them have the freedom to try and succeed, and especially to try and fail and try again.

This process of developing your child's inner advocate begins at birth, with your looking him in the eyes and really connecting when you talk. Doing this from the start, and throughout his life, lets him know he is loved and that he has your attention, but it also teaches him to read faces, to pick up on nonverbal clues, and to look at others directly when he wants to understand what they are saying and when he wants to use the full force of both body and verbal language to convey his own thoughts. To this day I still say "eyes on Mommy" to teach my son to use *all* of his senses when listening to me. My hope is he will remember to make eye contact when communicating with others too. It's a powerful trick I learned from one of Ronan's amazing karate instructors. When he said "eyes on coach," you could see the kids snap to attention, listening to his every word and watching his every movement. They were operating on all cylinders.

The process, of course, continues with more dialogue. When Ronan was a toddler I not only tried to model sound decision making, but I also explained many of my choices to him. Then I gradually began asking him to make choices of his own. To keep those early choices from being too overwhelming—and to prevent me from having to veto any of them—I used to offer two or three harmless options for him to choose from. For instance, I'd let him pick one toy from three of his favorites to take with him on long car rides. Other times I'd let him select any book from his library to read with me before bedtime. And after school he could always choose from a bunch of different healthy snacks. This way, I was always happy with his decision, whatever it was, and he was always thrilled to exercise his newfound independence and confidence. I wanted to avoid criticizing his selections as that only makes kids feel insecure and leads to them second-guessing their own judgment. That's why these controlled choices really work well early on.

Later I began asking him to explain his choices to me so he'd get used to expressing his likes and dislikes, needs and wants.

A common refrain in my house is "Use your words." I believe the more children experiment with language, the more they will understand and appreciate its depth, impact, and purpose. Experimenting with language includes thinking before speaking, choosing your words carefully, standing at a comfortable distance from the other person, and addressing them face to face. I want Ronan to know it is not just what he says that matters, but how he says it. Sometimes if he's struggling to access the right words we'll role-play. It's one thing to fix your child's problems for him and another to help him identify and use the tools in his toolbox the right way and at the right time. Role-play helps your children identify the tools available to them and to note that their own personal toolbox is filled with lots of different options.

The experts say that by the time children enter kindergarten or first grade they can actually begin to advocate for themselves with their teachers. If you receive a call from a teacher telling you that your child is talking instead of listening during story time, for instance, ask your child to tell you about her behavior during this time in class. Is she aware of what she is doing? Does she understand why her teacher might want everyone to be silent then? What might help her keep her thoughts to herself until the time is right for her to share them? Then encourage your child to speak with her teacher about her behavior directly. Role-playing can be effective here too because it helps children find the right words to apologize for and/or explain their actions the next day. What I like about role-playing is that it promotes thinking about the situation and your part in it, as well as planning for and developing a workable solution, instead of just rotely saying I'm sorry, which only teaches children to be people pleasers. *Suggesting that they speak on their own behalf lets children know you have faith in them, while practicing with them in this way reminds them that you still have their back.*

As Ronan gets older, I also encourage him to ask me for anything as long as he is prepared to build a solid case for it, just as my dad encouraged me. It was, by far, one of the best ways to teach me to present myself well.

If you're consistent in your messages, every now and then your children will let you know that they are picking up on your cues and learning how to advocate for themselves. Although I have to give you fair warning: it might not always be the way you had in mind. I remember when Ronan discovered what year I was born, it seemed like a long time ago to him. He started to get concerned about what might happen if I was no longer around. He came up with an idea. He decided he would stand in the center of FAO Schwarz until he saw the family that he wanted to go home with. And he told me he would point out all the toys he'd want to take with him. After assuring him I wasn't going anywhere, I actually thought to myself, "Oh my God. That's my boy. He's thinking ahead and he has a plan!"

Staying connected with your kids, helping them learn to connect with others, sharing your values with them at each stage of their development, letting them know that you expect them to live by those values too, and role-playing or strategizing possible ways to avoid, circumvent, or confront situations that challenge those values is how you actively advocate for your kids while teaching them to do so for themselves.

Among all of these suggestions, the one parents are apt to find the most difficult to do consistently is to model good advocacy and case-making skills themselves, even if they rock at doing it in other situations outside of the home. It is all too easy to resort to saying "because I said so" when confronted with resistance from your child on an issue that seems very clear-cut to you. You know, those times when you feel your parenting wisdom ought to override any and all objections, or when one more appeal on the same subject just cannot happen. I'm not saying that you can't exert some tough love and simply say no when a situation warrants it, nor am I saying that discussions won't get heated. That's life. You are going to get angry from time to time and you are going to have to play the I-know-best-card every once in a while, but that can't be the norm. *Parents need to keep the goal of raising their child into a wise, independent, strong, respectful, understanding, compassionate adult constantly in mind, and that means being all those things oneself.*

This extends to how you talk to everyone else in your family, not just your child. When my ex-husband Eric and I separated, we recognized that despite our differences we both wanted the very best for our son, whom we love so much. So we sat down and discussed what *the very best* really means and how we were going to make that happen as coparents. We knew a very essential part of the equation was modeling strong communication skills, so from that moment on, we really worked on how we interacted with each other. We took the time to relearn some of the skills that somehow became lax between us. As a result, the way we communicate now is really a positive example for Ronan. It's clear that we respect each other and that we're really and truly good *friends*. Remember, our children are watching and picking up cues from us all the time. The way parents sometimes speak with each other can send the wrong message. While it's generally important to be considerate of each other's views and to really listen and value what is being said, it is even more so in front of your kids.

By the way, as part of setting a good example for older children, it's okay to compromise in front of them from time to time—or sometimes even with them—to illustrate that the goal is not winning, the goal is figuring out what will best serve the situation and everyone involved. If, for instance, you are differing over an issue where compromise is possible, try asking, "What can I do to make this work for you? Is there something that's important to you that I can offer in return, because if so, I'd like to honor that request." This kind of give-and-take not only allows the other person to come back in loving graciousness and reciprocate the next time around, but it also suggests to them that just as in any other case-building situation, recognizing the other person's need and accounting for it in your request is vital. Making the other person feel validated is not only important to getting what you want, it's also essential to keeping the peace and maintaining mutual respect. When you resolve differences in front of your kids by seeking to find common-ground solutions, you are actually helping to raise a far better future advocate.

This thoughtful process is not only important when making requests, it's also imperative when discussing concerns or sharing criticism. Delivering both in a manner that also acknowledges the positive attributes in the person you're reasoning with models first-rate advocacy skills for your child. If you want someone else to be open to what you have to say, it's best not to start off or end the conversation by making him bristle. You will recall the concept of a love sandwich introduced in the earlier chapter on friendships; it is when you serve your critical message surrounded by positive statements, and you hold the judgment. Well, I'm here to tell you that while it works wonders with adults, it's even more effective with kids.

The great thing about consciously modeling these kinds of communication and advocacy skills for your children is that you improve your relationships with everyone else around you at the same time.

Whenever my dad spoke to me about the best way to raise children he'd always say, "Be involved. Be there. Be present. Listen. Sit down with your kids. Get right in front of them. Connect. Care. And don't be afraid to get mad. *Be passionate.*" He wasn't saying that we should shout and yell. He believed in the kind of considerate communication I just spoke about too. But he did mean that part about not being afraid to get mad. He really thought it was okay to get upset when a subject evoked strong emotion in us. He understood that getting angry is natural, but he would also tell us to learn to channel that anger—to try to figure out what was making us feel that way because he was convinced that when we do that we learn something important about ourselves, and he was right. After all, knowing ourselves, inside and out, is the first rule of self-advocacy. We can't be proactive on our own behalf if we don't know what it is that makes us tick, makes us happy, or spurs us on to want to confront challenges in life or to make a positive difference.

He'd also tell you that most kids need a little coaxing at first to become their own advocates. I've already given you examples of how he was my biggest cheerleader. I remember him always saying, "Hey, let's do this" or "Let's turn it on. Let's get after it," which was code for "Why don't you step outside of your comfort zone and try something new while I root for you from right over here."

The interesting thing—and something that I think is very relevant in our time—is that while he urged me to try new things and develop lots of different interests, he never overscheduled my day the way so many parents do today. When children are shuffled from one event to the next, they never have the time to think about or grow from what they just experienced. And if *you* chose all of their activities for them, they never get the chance to set priorities, plan, organize, or follow through on their own goals. My dear friend Shawn McSweeney, whom I mentioned earlier, reminded me the other day of something else my dad used to say on the subject. When Shawn and I first had our own kids, he'd tell us, "You're not doing it right unless it's boring." What he meant is that structure is really important; kids should be stimulated but not *over*stimulated. If your kids have a consistent routine, they always know what to expect. As they grow in confidence, they will begin to assert themselves naturally to expand those boundaries. And even if they do need a little encouragement to get to the next step, they'll be better prepared for making that leap because they are starting from a secure place. Whenever my dad did plan extra activities for us, he'd always involve us in the process. In retrospect, I realize how valuable that inclusion was. It helped us to be aware of our energies and how to use them best. Having a say then helped us practice for having even more of a say as an adult.

There is one more childhood story about teaching your children how to advocate for themselves that I'd like to share. It happened recently and was a real déjà-vu moment for me. My little boy is really good at building things. Because of this, we practically live at the hardware store. I even have a store card with my name on it. Imagine that! We're always buying nails, battery-operated screwdrivers, wood, Gorilla glue, and yes, ladies and gentlemen, we're also the proud, though careful, owners, of a hot-glue gun. When Ronan started attending a new school last fall, he was thrilled to see that one of the after-school electives was a woodshop class. The only challenge was that he had to be at least nine years old to enroll. Needless to say, he urgently wanted to be a part of this class and was very vocal about it. So I approached the director of the program and said, "This is his *specialty*. This is what he's really good at. It's his passion. His bliss. I want to make sure he can live it. I don't want to wait another year to get him into this class." That's when my mother's words came to me and I added, "Can you just give him a tryout?" It was as if I were Ronan's age again wanting to be a part of the boys' soccer team I told you about. I continued, "Please let him participate on the first day just to see if he can handle it. You can check to see if he's any good at it, if his fine motor skills and dexterity are there, and if he can follow directions and keep up with everybody else. If he can't go the distance, I'll trust your judgment and you can cut him from the class." Well, God bless this instructor—and the school—because they thought about it and gave my little eight-year-old the chance I asked for. After Ronan's first day I got the go-ahead to sign him up. Following my mom's example, I made the case for my son to have the *opportunity* to do something he loves. I didn't ask for a favor or an exception that wasn't warranted. I let Ronan know he had to earn it—and he did. I hope this lesson stays with him the way my mom's lesson did with me. What she did in that teachable moment was such a powerful thing that it still lingers in me to this day. It's in my blood. It's in my cells. It's part of who I am. This woodshop class presented an ideal opportunity for me to apply that same lesson to benefit my child. What an incredible example of life coming full circle.

CHAPTER 13

Making Divorce Work for Everyone Involved

I f you haven't already noticed the paradox running throughout this book, let me point it out for you now: while the entire premise is to show you how to get the things in life that serve you best, the key to getting those things, more often than not, lies in something my dad used to say all the time. In fact, I mentioned this principle in a different context earlier. He'd always tell us *"Don't make this life about you."* Just as I've recommended in previous chapters that you must factor in the needs of your future employer before you can prove that you are right for a job with them, or that you must explore the needs of your future spouse before you can be confident that you're entering a marriage where your own needs will be met, *I am telling you that when there are children involved in the dissolution of a marriage, advocating for them by putting their needs before your own is the only way to secure a healthy outcome for them and for yourself.*

I am glad that both of my divorces were amicable, but I am especially grateful that during the split from my son's father, he and I were committed to doing all that we could to ensure our son would continue to be happy and feel good about himself. We genuinely wanted him to know that he is loved. That is why we pursued an equal parenting partnership from the start. We recognized how important it is that our little guy continue to benefit from the strengths each of us brings to our relationship with him.

It makes me sad to see how often ego and pride get in the way of this process for some families. That kind of behavior is really harmful and damaging to children. I understand how traumatic a divorce can be, but aside from a situation where a child's safety is truly at risk, God should forbid any child from suffering because his parents could no longer live together or act as adults in each other's company.

There is one thing I wholeheartedly recommend to help you get to a place where you can set goals and follow through on making your child's needs a priority, and that is seeking the help of a family therapist from the outset of your divorce. Ours was terrific. She introduced us to the intricacies of coparenting and helped us establish a lifestyle that works well for us to this day.

First and foremost, family therapists can help you choose the best words to use when breaking the news. They can suggest age-appropriate responses to the kinds of questions children typically ask. They can even help you anticipate questions specific to your situation. Together you can prepare answers that are consistent and reassuring. Believe me, at times like these—no matter how good a talker you are—you can definitely find yourself at a loss for words—or worse, choosing all the *wrong* words. Because communication is so necessary, having someone who can help you find the right expression means everything.

Many counselors will advise you to tell your children together to signal that you are *still* a family. Doing this sends the important message that you will always have a *forever connection* to each other and that as parents you'll do everything in your power to end conflict and to ensure their happiness and well-being. To deepen this message, my former husband and I both keep pictures of the other parent in our respective homes, and we still refer to ourselves as family.

In the early stages of divorce, counselors also teach you to provide a kind of *no-fault assurance* for your child. Kids will naturally assume responsibility for what is happening in their home. They equate taking responsibility with taking control. Under circumstances in which they feel they have virtually *no* control, they will try to fix whatever is broken. If they can't fix it, they often believe they did something wrong or that they neglected to do something that could have changed everything. No child should ever have to carry that kind of weight around—consciously or unconsciously. It's important to be as clear as possible that your breakup is not their fault. State it as strongly as you can using all the tools of persuasive communication you've learned throughout this book, including voice intonation, eye contact, and body language to drive that message home. Cuddle, console, and assure them they did absolutely nothing wrong.

I love the expression *Keep calm and carry on* as it totally applies here too. When a child's life is changing so rapidly, a sense of stability becomes that much more important to them. We've learned to minimize change, and when it does have to occur we now know to establish new and consistent routines in the place of old ones.

Another piece of advice I appreciated and am now passing on to you is this: remember to validate your child's feelings. First, be sure to lavish them with lots of love. Let them know that they mean the world to you. Tell them often that you love them, then tell them again. And do so with your actions as well as with your words. But in those moments when they still feel sad, let them have those emotions. It is only when they express themselves that you can truly address the complex feelings they are grappling with. Since validating another person's perspective communicates acceptance, it's especially important at vulnerable times like these that you really listen to your children's concerns, summarize what you've heard them say, and even anticipate how they may be feeling before they express those thoughts themselves. They should never feel as if they need to mask their emotions or try to be someone else so they can keep peace and some semblance of order in their new situation.

One silver lining to this kind of major life event is that if you guide your children in the right way, they can truly learn to understand and manage their emotions under any circumstances. It's hard to imagine this now, but if you make this a teachable moment, you will be giving your children the lifelong gift of emotional resilience.

It also helps to put your best face forward. Going to work and socializing in addition to taking care of your health, appearance, and your home signals to your children that you are okay, that they will also adjust to their new reality, and that there can still be quality of life even when there is change and upheaval. The added benefit of this approach is that when you engage in life, life engages you . . . and when you look better, you feel better too. As you socialize, it is important to make sure that your friends and family know the ground rules as well. You want everyone in your life to be mindful of your children's needs and to be completely onboard with the specifics and the philosophy of your coparenting plan so they can reinforce the environment of mutual cooperation and respect you are fostering. Don't let any hurt they feel on your behalf influence your children. With their help you can all heal faster.

Although I've used the term *coparenting* several times already, it may be useful to define it a little more clearly for those of you who are new to the concept. It is both a philosophy and a practice based on the notion that it's your child's birthright to have a meaningful relationship with both of his parents. It demands that you and your former spouse wipe the slate clean, putting all past differences behind you so that you can focus primarily on maintaining respective but equal relationships with your child. The initial process involves creating an actual parenting plan that clearly lays out expectations and a code of conduct so everyone begins and remains on the same page. Coparenting plans are written on an individual basis, as each family's circumstances are different. A family therapist can work with you and your lawyers or mediator to help you draft and adhere to an equitable plan. On a very basic level, these plans help to establish fair schedules, consistent household and discipline rules, and financial and educational guidelines as well as specifics on how to handle emergencies so all parties remain informed and involved. On a broader scale, they help define the larger life tenets you both wish to instill in your child.

I have to say that while everyone's experience is different, the benefits of coparenting have been enormous for us. It really does provide us with a chance to impact our son's life equally. You can see it more clearly after the dust settles and you are able to assert some objectivity. For instance, there are qualities my ex-husband has that I am genuinely glad my son continues to share in. Eric, much like my father, has a kind of charm that reminds me of old Hollywood, but he is still very real and down to earth. He is sophisticated, smart, and athletic; loves to read; and is attentive to the kinds of details that escape a lot of other people. These are wonderful qualities for Ronan to observe and strive for. It's also widely evident that Ronan has inherited his father's creativity and love of design. Having a close relationship with his dad will no doubt help these interests continue to flourish. Someday I'm sure Ronan will appreciate the way his dad has reimagined and reshaped his three-generation-old family business, making lots of environmentally sound decisions, and how for a time in the fashion world he put programs in place to support new and emerging designers in a very difficult and competitive field. Some of these designers, including Proenza Schouler and Derek Lam among others, have since gone on to achieve tremendous success. These kinds of actions demonstrate to our son the importance of not just doing things you are passionate about, but of doing them in a way that truly helps others. Our kids need as many examples of positive advocacy as they can get and who better to get it from than both of their parents? *We always hope our children will inherit our best traits, but coparenting ensures they'll have the chance to witness, absorb, and emulate them too.*

It may not be possible to put aside your differences with your ex or to admit to his finer points any time soon, but if it is, doing so can enhance all of your lives and can model for your child the kind of cooperation required at every level of effective advocacy.

Of course, divorce affects *everyone* in a family, not just our children. Deep bonds of love and respect form between in-laws too. My father was greatly saddened when my first marriage ended, and while he was not alive when my second marriage ended, I know he would have had deep compassion for all of us in that situation too. He was very close to the Villency family. He loved them all. In the end, though, I know he would have been very proud of how Eric and I crafted a new parenting dynamic for the benefit of our son. One of the most pleasant results of coparenting is that Eric and I are better friends and communicators than ever. It has served to strengthen our relationship and our bond and is noticeable to us as well as to others.

My dad was someone who believed you should always seek the advice of experts in all matters of life. He would tell anyone going through a divorce that there is no shame in seeking help—legal, financial, or emotional—at any time in life, but especially at a time like this. Even under normal circumstances, lots of people cringe at the thought of turning outward for support or advice because they believe doing so shows weakness. They take pride in being independent and strong-minded, so when they really do feel fragile, the last thing they want to do is reveal those insecurities to another person. As so many of us who have endured divorce know, the end of a marriage brings with it a profound sense of sorrow, and for some people a feeling of failure too. But my dad would tell you to get over it—to move on. He'd tell you that failure is when you don't take the opportunity to correct a situation with all the resources available to you in the big, wide, knowledgeable world around you. So listen to his advice. Pick yourself up and prove to yourself—and your children if you have them—that moving forward even after the greatest disappointments can be an incredibly empowering experience.

CHAPTER 14

Avoiding Family Drama

Have you ever wished you took just one more second to think before you spoke? That you'd just bitten your tongue? Or maybe, there was a time when you regretted *not* saying what was on your mind?

There are occasions in life when we advocate too much for a loved one, and other times when we don't advocate enough. Both occasions can lead to drama. In the case of overadvocating, the person offering advice sees their behavior as supportive, while the receiver often perceives this as meddling. And haven't we all inadvertently, yet lovingly, interfered a time or two in the lives of the people closest to us?

I've already mentioned my younger brother, Anthony, several times in this book, but I'm not sure I've told you what an accomplished individual he is. He's supersmart and talented. I don't often have an occasion to describe the person he's grown up to be, but when I do, it's clear that he's pretty awesome. He possesses so many of my mother's artistic traits, including a skill for painting. He's also inherited my father's beautiful voice. My father actually sang with Frank Sinatra. His voice was legendary.

Anthony also shares my father's business acumen. Whatever he does, he excels at. He's currently vice president of North American Sales for Rockstar Energy Drinks and he is every bit a rock star in my book. My brother is someone who knows his voice. He's comfortable in his own skin. He's strong-minded and direct. He is never one to be taken advantage of, but he's also a great listener and excellent at working with others to achieve common goals. I often ask him to weigh in on decisions I am making because I value what he has to say. His opinions are always well thought out. He's a great brother and truly a best friend. He's been a real pillar of strength for me in times of need. But despite his current success and his many great abilities, there are times when I find myself reverting to the relationship we had as kids. It's hard not to still fill the older sister role and fuss over him.

I know I'm not the only person who has done this. Lots of older siblings behave this way with their younger siblings well into adulthood. And parents do it all the time too—even when their children are responsible enough to raise kids of their own. There are also some people who do this with their more carefree and adventurous childhood friends even though these friends have settled down, earned advanced degrees, and are flourishing in their careers. It's hard for people to switch gears and change the role they've played for years with a loved one. *But one way of advocating for the people you care about when the urge to add your two cents comes over you is to examine whether your behavior is warranted or if it is born out of habit? And is the need really theirs or yours?*

In my case, I helped to raise Anthony since he was eight. I was not only the older sister; I was also a mother figure in many ways. Of course, my father was a very hands-on dad. Despite how hard he worked, he was always deeply involved in everything we did. But because I saw him doing so much for us and sometimes exhausting himself in the process, I tried to help by watching over Anthony too. You can see how worrying about my brother became instinctive. I can't help but look out for him. But what I learned from all this mother-henning is that at some point in everyone's life, age differences cease to mean that you know more or have greater experience than the other person.

In some families, it's not even about being older or supposedly wiser. The sibling who has always been a straight arrow might still think he knows what's best for the brother or sister who tends to make out-of-the-box choices. If you fit any of these profiles, check yourself. You may be contributing to family drama even though your actions, in your mind, are a reflection of how much you care. It all comes down to this: the best way to advocate for the people you love as you grow and mature and have independent lives is to simply let them know you are there for them if they need you. Respect them for who they've become. Trust them to make sound decisions and to be their own best advocate. You can express your opinions, but do so as an equal and a friend rather than as an authority figure. When you do this you are letting them know you're a trustworthy sounding board, and that they have your unconditional love and support.

Of course, that doesn't mean you shouldn't be honest when family members ask for your help or opinion. You owe it to them to tell it like it is.

There may be other times when you must weigh the uncertainty of not speaking your mind against the responsibility and guilt you may shoulder if you don't tell the truth about how you feel. Honesty can cause rifts or hurt people's feelings or offend them, but you never want to regret failing to give the tough love because you didn't have the strength or courage. In those difficult situations, stop and think about the fabric and history of your relationship. Dig deep to find a balanced response. *Advocacy, as I have said many times before, is about really knowing the people you are dealing with, putting yourself in their shoes, and truly appreciating their perspective. It's also about knowing the most opportune time and place to share your opinions.* If you feel you have considered all these factors, then go ahead and give them your advice. Tell them what you think because they deserve your thoughtful perspective as the person who has their best interests at heart. Then trust them to hear what you're saying, take it into account, and to ultimately do what's in their heart because in the end it is their choice. Not everyone is going to have the same viewpoints as you. You can't assume that something that would be right for you would be right for someone else, no matter how much DNA or collective memory you share. And after you've said your piece, know when to stand down, ease off, and say, "All right, let me see how this plays out." If you don't crowd or overwhelm your loved ones or exert emotional ownership over them, if you don't demand that they take your advice, and if you honor their right to independent thought and action, they'll come to you when they need help because they know you'll see the gray (not just the black and white) of an issue. They'll know you're willing to concede ground in order to help them find what works best for them. That is truly the way to stand behind them and live a drama-free life.

For many people, another relationship that can be fraught with drama is the one we have with our in-laws. Once again, important familial roles are shifting. Problems can occur when the newcomer tries too hard—or not hard enough—to fit in.

Advocating for a welcome and secure place in your in-laws' heart and home requires observing and understanding the dynamic of the family and their history, traditions, and idiosyncrasies. It means taking cues before leaping in and claiming a spot and recognizing that parents and siblings relate to one another in their own way. When you come along, things naturally change. The emotional pie is suddenly divided differently. But when you are sincere and patient, families do ultimately understand that the village can grow, and that the emotional pie can grow as well, feeding everyone. Being respectful of those who came before you and recognizing that other family members have been in your loved one's life a lot longer than you, can really make a difference. As the new kid on the block, pick up on the cues his or her family gives you. Be warm and open from the start, but take a gradual approach to inserting yourself into their activities, especially family joking. Don't be overzealous or demand immediate affection or acceptance. There is no need to rush in and take charge. Sometimes sitting back and letting things unfold naturally is your best bet.

I also think it's important to be yourself (your *best* self) because people respond well to authenticity. And another tenet of mine is to always show respect toward your loved one's parents. The way you treat them is an indication of how well you treat their child, and in time how well you'll treat their grandchildren too. If parents see that you are good to their son or daughter, you're going to have their love and respect for life because what everyone wants most for their child is happiness. Show them how crazy you are about your partner—how content and well loved he is—and you will be embraced as if you are their child too.

If you've married into a family with discord, you still have to make an effort to get along. You still have to try to make that difference. You still have to advocate for a good, solid, warm, and loving relationship with each person who is important to your loved one. Anything less than a genuine effort to bond with your partner's family is going to cause drama at some point, so start off on the right footing.

Friends tell me I struck gold in the in-law department not once but twice, and they're right. I enjoyed wonderful relationships with Gavin's mother and father, and have an especially loving connection with Eric's parents to this day. I am fortunate to be very close to Bob and Rowann Villency, their daughter, Cara, who is like a sister to me, and their son-in-law, Josh Sacks. They are all extraordinarily good people, but one reason why we've developed such a strong bond is because *I really wanted to*. I value family and know the definition of that can extend well beyond blood relatives. I've always believed that such important people in your loved one's life should be important to you too. You have to treat them like your own family and extend a sincere heart at all times. Know that loving your spouse's family is one of the best ways you can advocate for their happiness, your happiness, and the happiness of your future children too!

I have no doubt what my dad would say on the subject of avoiding family drama. My father believed family, in all its different forms, is the greatest treasure in the world. And this is from a man who had been separated by an ocean from his family in Ireland for decades, endured the loss of his wife at a young age, raised two children on his own, and spent years fostering a surrogate family from the most amazing array of people he knew. He'd tell you to keep your family close; never let the differences between you grow disproportionately to your love for each other; make every effort to keep the peace because, as the saying goes, "It is easier to keep love alive than it is to rebuild trust," and, finally, to expand your family to include all who are deserving of a place in your heart. It is pure and simple advice, but oh so wise.

CHAPTER 15

Caring for Aging Parents

Sadly, I know what it is like to lose a parent at a young age and I know what it is like to lose a parent after living a full and wonderful life with them. It is incredibly difficult under both circumstances, but the latter comes with an added complication. You not only have to deal with the pain of watching your aging parent slip away, but you also have the responsibility of shouldering their medical treatment. When you advocate for a loved one under these serious conditions, you can't help but wonder if you are doing all that is possible. You pray you haven't left one stone unturned, while at the same time you pray you have and that you'll find that stone—and the cure beneath it—in the nick of time the way it sometimes happens in the movies.

As I mentioned earlier, my father had esophageal cancer. By the time it was diagnosed it had already progressed to stage-four cancer. The doctors told us he would live for just three to twelve more weeks. We were advised to give him only palliative care. He was the rock of our world and we would have done anything to prolong his life, provided it didn't cause him any further pain. Like so many other families who receive this kind of news, we threw ourselves into an investigative process to see what other possible forms of care were out there. We reached out to MD Anderson, Memorial Sloan Kettering, Mount Sinai, Columbia-New York Presbyterian, California Pacific Medical Center in San Francisco, and UCSF Medical Center among other hospitals renowned for their success rate and innovative practices. We looked into aggressive treatments, alternative treatments, and we also contacted anyone and everyone who was conducting further studies on the disease. We were doing what my dad had always taught us to do when faced with a challenge, when fighting for a cause: we were seeking answers from the people who knew best. It not only led us to consult with top doctors throughout the United States, but it also led us to talk with physicians in the UK and Japan, where some interesting research in this particular type of cancer was being done. We tried to learn as much as we could as fast as we could since we had such a narrow window of time. People were so generous and forthcoming with their knowledge that the experience is what drives my work with the Esophageal Cancer Education Foundation to this day. It's important to share new findings on the chance that they can help one more person survive or live longer than their expectancy.

Because of the thoroughness of our search, we ended up with some of the best medical professionals in their respective fields. We are indebted to Dr. Jaffer Ajani at MD Anderson, Dr. Alan Kramer and Dr. Natalie Bzowej, both at California Pacific Center, and to our dear friend Dr. Laurie Green, who referred us to Dr. Kramer and Dr. Bzowej. We are eternally and immeasurably grateful for the great care and love these fine doctors showed us. They represent the very best the medical profession has to offer.

The same is true for the nursing staff, in particular Pat Lateef, who is also the mother of my law school friend Mike Lateef.

While we were looking at all the different medical options, my dad advocated in his own way by setting a significant goal for himself: he vowed to live until my son's second birthday. Keeping a milestone like this in mind helps give patients purpose and focus. Remember, all advocacy requires that you hold your objective clearly in your mind. While we hoped for a cure or a miracle, the objective was to extend his quality time with family as long as we could. He followed the advice of the different specialists we saw. He underwent every test he was asked to take and he endured every suggested treatment. He also made every moment of his last months count, just as he did the rest of his life. He flirted with the nurses who gave him such good care and made the attendants laugh whenever he could. Somehow he managed to overcome the indignities of dying and made us see some of its graces too.

True to his determined nature, he defied the doctor's predictions and lived for fourteen more months. He had made his case with God to live long enough to see Little Buddy turn two and God heard him. He celebrated my son's second birthday on October 4th as he promised he would. During that time he even taught Ronan how to walk—it only took him one day.

In retrospect, I realized that those fourteen months were also long enough for him to be sure Anthony and I would be okay. He died, symbolically in many ways, on Thanksgiving night. He was always a grateful man, and he often told my brother and me how honored he was to have been our dad. He shared these sentiments one last time on that night. He was at peace when he took my hand and let us know that he wasn't worried about us and that he didn't want us to worry either. Knowing that we possessed all the love, wisdom, common sense, strength, and courage he could give us and that we could take care of ourselves and each other, he thanked us and told us he was proud of us. Then we said the Our Father prayer together and before taking his last breath he simply said, "My job is done. Good-bye my loves."

I discovered a lot on my health-care journey with my amazing dad and am sharing what I learned hoping that it will help us all advocate better for a generation that has certainly advocated for us. As our parents age they deserve guardian angels, and who better to fill that role than their children? Many are not getting the care that they need and it is up to us to help them find it.

First, what was confirmed for me is that communication is your number one advocacy tool and best friend when dealing with the medical world. It is crucial when interacting with your parent, their doctors, your siblings, and with everyone else who cares about them.

Even before illness sets in, talking with your parents about their health and how they are caring for themselves is vital. One of the realities that shocks me most is how infrequently older patients see a doctor. They are supposed to be the responsible generation—the ones who always do their due diligence. But many of them are uncharacteristically lax when it comes to maintaining their health. So start advocating for your parents early by asking if they are going for their annual physical. If they are being treated for a chronic illness, also double check to be sure they are seeing their specialist on a more regular basis. Don't assume that they are. I understand that they avoid doctors like the plague because they are reluctant to hear any potential bad news. Ignorance really can be bliss sometimes. If no one is telling them to slow down because of some health constraint, they can just go on about their merry business. Avoidance is a positive thing in their mind. I also understand that the reason the oldest of patients fail to make regular wellness visits is a logistical one. They often can't get to and from the doctor's office on their own. Maintaining independence means not asking anyone else to get them where they are going. But remind them that maintaining their health is what ensures independence. No matter how much you sympathize with their reasons, you must insist that they make these visits anyway. If you have to, help schedule their appointments, accompany them, or arrange for their travel. AARP provides a state-by-state guide to transportation assistance for those who can no longer drive or take public transportation. The American Public Transportation Association can help too, and in many states information is available by calling 511.

If your parent neglects to seek or receive the right preventive care or have regular checkups, the diagnosis of some very easy-to-treat conditions can be missed—or worse, these conditions can escalate over time into full-blown or fatal diseases. You can't imagine how many patients dismiss heartburn without realizing that it is an early warning sign of esophageal cancer. However, regular visits don't always help us avoid crises—my father was someone who was vigilant about his health his whole life. He wanted to make sure that as a single parent he would always be there for my brother and me. He exercised every day regardless of whether he was tired or had a long day. He was in outstanding health and shape, he didn't smoke, and he never experienced acid reflux or heartburn, which are early warning signs of his disease. He also regularly and religiously saw his primary care physician. He monitored his health closely with cardio checks and even colonoscopies. Unfortunately, he never had an endoscopy of his esophagus or stomach because he was symptom free so his doctor never ordered it, as these procedures are not done without cause. But, in many cases, regular visits can catch a brewing problem early. Just having regular blood tests can tell us a lot. Even though my dad had done everything right, we discovered that his cancer was caused by *Helicobacter pylori* bacterium (otherwise known as

H. pylori infection), a silent and deadly cancer precursor that he had somehow been exposed to at some point in his life. *H. pylori* infection causes chronic inflammation of the inner lining of the stomach and is most likely acquired by ingesting contaminated food and water. More than 50 percent of the world's population is infected with it, yet roughly 80 percent are asymptomatic. It's worth getting tested as a simple round of antibiotics could help you get rid of it before it poses any problems.

Another way to advocate for an aging parent is to find him a good geriatric doctor. Just as you would take your young child to a pediatrician or your teenage daughter to a gynecologist, you need to be sure that your aging parent is seeing a doctor who understands his very specific stage of life too. All too often, ailments are written off by both the patient and his general practitioner as simply facets of old age. It's the catchall category for most symptoms experienced by this demographic the same way that stress is the catchall for the rest of us. What your parent needs at this time in his life is a doctor who understands all of his health-care needs and investigates all of his ailments. A doctor who specializes in geriatric care understands how your parent's physical activity, nutrition, and emotional well-being impact the multiple conditions most elderly patients have because he is trained to. Geriatric doctors also understand how the many different medications these conditions require interact with one another and they can help monitor the mix of drugs your parent is prescribed. Just as in any other situation we've discussed so far, when your parent feels as if he is being listened to and heard he is more likely to be an active agent in his own care. Constructive dialogue can be resumed between these patients and their doctors. Older patients may be more willing to share details of their symptoms and reactions and get the guidance they need if they believe doing so will help rather than hamper them. Instead of halting medications without telling their doctor every time the dose or combinations makes them feel bad, the hope is they will talk with their doctors about possible ways to remedy the situation. Who knows, with this kind of specialist on their side, older patients may finally be included in clinical trials for the various medications they take. After all, the elderly are among the largest user groups of prescription drugs. Seeing a geriatric doctor who understands their unique challenges can potentially give these patients their voice back and enable them to advocate more effectively for themselves.

Because of the rising age of baby boomers, geriatrics is becoming an increasingly popular specialty and more and more centers for the care of the aged are cropping up. It is much easier to find the kind of ongoing help your parent needs than it has ever been before, so make the extra effort. When you do meet with this kind of specialist, or any other doctor new to your parent's care, bring your parent's medical history with you. This includes all the conditions or illnesses he has been treated for in the past and is being treated for presently. Also come armed with the contact information for any doctors who may have recently seen or treated your parent and the names of the medications he is presently taking. Specify whether it is in the generic or brand form and also note the current doses. If your parent has taken tests recently, be sure to have the test results with you as well. By the way, everyone should take this kind of checklist with them whenever they see a new doctor, no matter what their age. Although digital records exist everywhere these days and can be shared relatively easily, requests for a transfer of files can still take a few days. Having your medical history handy speeds the process along, keeps you from taking expensive or unnecessary tests twice, and begins a pattern of good communication between you and your new physician. It also eases your parent's anxiety about continuity of care.

While I hope your parents are with you for a very long time, if you are ever told that your parent has a terminal condition as I was, know that communication becomes that much more important.

I was very fortunate that my brother and I were both there to advocate for my dad in his final months. We were in constant touch with each other, we made decisions large and small together, and we both did whatever we possibly could to ease his mind and his pain. We were each better at doing different things for him so those were the tasks we focused on. I may have been the one to give my dad his meals through his feeding tube because that was just too emotionally hard on my brother, but in the end it was Anthony who carried the day. I will never forget how, after helping to care for my dad, he turned his attention to caring for me too. Anthony was the adult, the one who was the giver then, because I was also caring for my little boy. I was the one who gave the eulogy but it was Anthony who flew back and forth between LA and San Francisco to sell my dad's home, to pack up his personal effects, and to send me whatever he thought I needed or wanted. There was this dollhouse my father made for me by hand after my mother died to help cheer me up and take my mind off the incredible loss we'd all just sustained. Anthony wrapped it up so carefully and sent it to New York by freight knowing how important it was to me. In the way you usually ask Jesus to take the wheel at times like that, it was Anthony who had taken the wheel for me.

We were also lucky to have other loved ones there to support us and to share in the caregiving too. We cannot thank Judith, my father's second wife, whom he married later in life, and her wonderful children, Greg and Lisa, enough for being there with us every step of the way despite having been divorced from my dad for several years. It meant so much to all of us that they were by our side and in our corner.

I'm aware, however, that it doesn't always work like this. There can be contention in some families over who is doing most of the caregiving when a loved one is ill. Siblings can often get upset with one another, and speak out of frustration or anger, which only breaks down the lines of communication at a time when that skill is needed most. It seems to me that the best you can do if you feel others are not stepping up and carrying their fair share of the load is to make a direct appeal to them without judgment. Be specific about what you need them to do. If they cannot do what you want, ask them what they *are* able to do. If they still don't rise to the occasion, continue to keep them informed of what is happening without any pressure. Each person handles stress, worry, and grief differently. I use the word grief because people really do mourn the once-vital parent they grew up with when they see them in diminished health. This emotion can be experienced well before a parent passes. Your sibling may simply not be capable of helping out initially, but ongoing communication gives her plenty of opportunity to accept what is happening and to do something about it. We each have a different relationship with our parents. It's important to remember that we all don't always give in the same way. Criticizing a sibling may only immobilize her more, rather than inspire participation. Relay details often enough for her to see that her help is needed. Advocating means *fighting for* not *fighting with*. As I've said before in many different ways, you have to make your case in a manner that makes other people listen, and that usually means considering their needs as well as your own. You may feel as if your parents' needs take precedence over your sibling's—and they do—but this more communicative approach is likely to get more traction than making people defensive ever does.

One great way to keep all of your family and friends posted is through a service called CarePages. They are a secure online community that provides free websites for people facing life-changing health events. Through them you can communicate news on your loved one's progress to all those who need or want to know. Posting something for friends and family on a regular basis allows those at a distance to stay informed, and it keeps you from having to return tons of emails or phone calls when your focus needs to be elsewhere. It also serves as a daily record of what transpired, which you can refer to when speaking with the doctors or others involved directly in the patient's care. Days and events tend to blur together when you are under duress, so a log like this really helps. It also allows you to receive emotional support from others in your own time. Reading messages of concern and care while your loved one is taking tests or when they are sleeping can be very comforting. Because you are keeping people apprised, those who want to help will have a better and more specific idea of what support is most needed. Their offers of assistance can be that much more specific and useful. Keeping the channels open often means you don't have to go it alone. Even if some family members disappoint you, other people, including some you least expect, often come forward to help.

When a diagnosis like this is rendered, another way to advocate for your parent is to decide together which options, if any, you will explore. It's a tough conversation to have, but ask them what they are really up for. Figure out together if you'll look into every available alternative, or if you'll go the more conventional route. If your parent is willing to participate in studies or try new medicines, then let the doctors know so they can steer you in the direction of the most promising courses of treatment. This is a complex consideration, so don't assume you know how your parent will respond.

Before he decides on anything, though, urge him to seek second opinions. I'm on TV programs where diverse opinions matter and prove their importance every day. The same is true in the medical field. Different people have different perspectives and different experiences. Seeking as much input as possible will only help to better inform you and give you more options. Cast a wide net—ask friends, neighbors, and anyone else who has endured and survived this condition to tell you which doctors and treatments helped them most. It's easy to just get bogged down by the weight of the news, but try not to let that happen. It's important to get as complete a perspective on the disease as you possibly can as early as you can. In addition to consulting all these people, be sure to reach out to the organizations specifically formed to disseminate information about the disease you are dealing with. Many people are under the misimpression that these groups exist primarily to raise funds for research, but many of them act as facilitators too. The Esophageal Cancer Education Foundation (ECEF) was an extraordinary help to my family. This organization, and so many other nonprofit health organizations like it, communicate valuable new findings, offer practical advice, and provide a variety of other services, including referrals to the best doctors and treatment programs. Some even help resolve insurance or Medicare challenges and arrange for payment plans as costs mount. And talk about advocating—a fair share of these organizations have survivors on staff who really get what you are going through. In fact, ECEF was founded by a survivor. His name is Bart Frazzitta and he is another personal hero of mine. These people's input is priceless.

Finally, I understand that the hardest thing is knowing when to let go, especially when you are a hopeful and determined person, when you have been raised as I have to make your best case, fight the good fight, and pursue every possible option. There was a point at which I was called back to San Francisco from New York because my dad's condition had declined so severely it appeared that he would pass at any moment. As I was rushing to the airport, I called my brother to see how he was doing. Anthony told me that he had just said, "I'm okay. I'm waiting for Kimberly." When I arrived two wonderful priests who had known my dad and were close to our family for many years, Father Mario Preitto and Father Stephen Privett, administered last rites. Miraculously, my dad seemed to rally. Palliative care physicians will tell you that there is a phenomenon wherein a terminal patient will suddenly experience renewed energy and lucidity. That period gave me hope that there was still more we could do for him. When he began to decline again I was riddled with angst about whether there was one last thing we could try. I was looking for that Hail Mary pass. I just couldn't let go. But I am grateful my dad's lifelong and powerful philosophy was ultimately there to guide me once more. He strongly believed that if you lived your life with conscience, meaning, and care; if you were thoughtful, kind, and generous in your daily interactions with people; and if you considered all perspectives of an issue, you can depart this world with peace in your soul when your time inevitably comes. There will be no list of things you wish you would have said or done differently. As I wrestled with whether I had made my best case to the doctors, whether I asked all the right questions and explored all possible avenues, there was a profound moment when I simply knew that I had. It came when my father gave my brother and me the most loving gift a parent can give a child. He held our hands and said with such tranquility and calm, "I have no regrets. I've lived a great life and I have two of the best kids in the world." With those words he soothed us. He gave us his blessing and permission to free him. This is by far the greatest example of why the process of making your case, considering the perspective of others, and living your life with purpose and integrity is so important to me and why I wish to share it with you.

CHAPTER 16

Help! How to Ask for It, Receive It, and Give It

I can't believe we've arrived at the final chapter already. Most of you came to this book hoping to better exercise your voice; to learn how to be stronger; and to articulate, pursue, and get what you want and need in life. In many ways you were hoping to learn how to become more independent. The great irony, as you've probably discovered along the way, is that the quickest way to become more self-sufficient is to actually ask for help. One of the more frequent mantras of this book is that you don't ask just *anyone* for help . . . you ask people who know more than you do.

You will recall that in the very first chapter I talked about internships for this reason. But learning from others should never be relegated to just the early part of your career. It is something you should do continually throughout your life. You should feel free to attend seminars; read books, magazines, and newspapers;

and comb the Internet to keep track of people who blog on subjects that interest you and to dialogue with everyone you meet.
You should seek mentors at every stage of life and career, and if
you are ever so fortunate to reach the pinnacle of your field, look
to your right and to your left and seek the company and perspective of your accomplished peers too. It's what Steven Spielberg,
Oprah Winfrey, Warren Buffett, and Bill Gates continue to do,
and many others too. You can learn something of value from so
many different people. Think about how the Ted Conference was
born, or how the World Leaders Conference, the Young Presidents Organization, and the World Presidents Organization first
came into existence. Seeking additional knowledge is always ad-
mirable, as long as it is preceded with forethought and preparation, self-awareness, and a healthy respect for the other person's
position, time, and perspective.

By picking up this book, you have already advocated for yourself in a significant way. I hope it addressed many of your questions and that it inspires you to continue to seek answers from
other people who have a different frame of reference, lots of experience, or a wealth of new ideas to share. Experts are people who
were once filled with lots of questions too, and many still are, so
they respect the exploratory process. As a journalist, I sometimes
feel as if my questions will never end. I know other curious people
feel the same way. *Yet one of the biggest impediments to successful
self-advocacy is a fear of asking for help.* All too many people see
it as a weakness. The real weakness, however, is failing to make
or take the opportunity to fast track your growth by seeking out
those who can help you.

If fear is keeping you from taking the next step and turning
all this advice into definitive action, then consider this: studies
show that people overestimate how many folks they would have
to approach before one agrees to give them help by as much as

50 percent. In other words, your odds of getting valuable input from people who can truly help you are far better than you may think.

The true test of how well you use the advice and stories you've found here hinges on how well you grasp the concept that whether you are advocating for yourself or someone else, the process always involves the consideration and participation of others. Even *self-made* millionaires had to rely on people to embrace and buy their goods or services. Even responsible, disciplined, go-getter me—who ran a household and juggled schoolwork, extracurricular activities, and several part-time jobs as a teenager—needed and relied on the help of a whole community of friends and family to get where I am today. I still need an entourage of people to keep things flowing smoothly in my life. It really does take a village. So to be the best advocate you can be, don't be scared to embrace the idea of pursuing, receiving, and giving help more completely.

Before appealing to someone for assistance, admit to yourself that you need it. You never want to ask for or accept help begrudgingly or halfheartedly. When you frame your need clearly to yourself and others it wildly improves your chances of getting what you're asking for. Whatever you do, don't make people guess what it is you need from them, or expect them to just offer it on their own. If you don't know how to ask for it, it may appear as if you won't know what to do with their help when you receive it.

And try not to let the fear that you may run up *favor debt* paralyze you either. Trust that the person's help and your own drive and perseverance will ultimately put you in a place to reciprocate in some way. There are many ways to show your gratitude. As you rise in your field, crediting the people who helped you is one way. Supporting a special interest of theirs is another. If you can't make a monetary donation to a favorite cause of theirs, volunteer your time. And send equally interesting and accomplished people their way when you think there is a potential connection, per our earlier discussion of networking.

On the subject of giving help to others, all I can say is that while it often begins out of a sense of obligation, you'd be surprised how much satisfaction and joy you will feel in the end. I can't tell you how gratifying I've found *giving back* to be over the years. I choose my philanthropic pursuits selectively so my energies can yield the greatest good. I recognize that I can't do everything, so I opt to concentrate on the things I *can* do. I especially try to support work that has an impact on many people at once. Some of my true advocacy heroes are those who have the foresight and the skills to mobilize large groups of people behind a goal that might otherwise seem insurmountable.

My admiration runs deep for a woman named Etta Agnell Wheeler. She was a church worker, who more than 140 years ago had the compassion, drive, and determination to not only help a young child whose foster mother was mistreating her, but to also raise the world's awareness of violence against kids and to rally against it. In the absence of any other formal resources, Etta approached the American Society for the Prevention of Cruelty to Animals for help. It's astonishing to think that prior to her actions no equivalent organization existed *anywhere in the world* to advocate for abused and neglected children, but a stellar one existed to help animals. With the aid of Henry Bergh, the founder of the ASPCA, and his legal counsel, Eldridge Thomas Gerry, the New York Society for the Prevention of Cruelty to Children was born. It is the world's oldest child protection agency. Since then, countless children have benefited from the services it provides, including mental health counseling and legal and educational guidance. There are too many children who can't advocate for themselves. They truly need us to do it for them. On my own, I could only help one child at a time. But supporting an esteemed organization like this ensures the well-being of many vulnerable abused and neglected children, extending protection to them through tougher and enforceable legal means that would not be available to them without this organization's existence. I'm incredibly honored to have received the Strength of Our Society Award from the NYSPCC and continually pleased to sit on its Children's Council. My hat is off to Executive Director Mary Pulido, whose fearless advocacy is unparalleled. I admire her greatly for her unrelenting and tenacious fight on behalf of children.

I'm also proud to personally support the scholarship fund of the Navy SEAL Foundation. Those involved in naval special warfare continue to sacrifice and risk so much for our country. They can be away from home and family for more than 270 days a year on the most dangerous of missions. It is important to support them and their families— especially the children of fallen soldiers —and to alleviate the kinds of stress they endure, including the financial pressures of paying for their children's education. What I love about any scholarship program is that it ultimately empowers the recipients. *In the spirit of true advocacy, it is all about giving others the tools to help themselves.*

And just as I support the Esophageal Cancer Education Foundation in honor of my father, I am a supporter of the Francis Pope Memorial Foundation. This organization helps to meet the financial and emotional needs of families with a sick child, many of whom are suffering from cancer. My mother was an ardent supporter of children in need, and, of course, she also suffered the ravages of leukemia, which is a cancer of the blood cells that affects children too. Supporting such efforts has been a passion of mine since the day my mother died. I find the story of this organization's origins very moving, and the work they continue to do thirty-three years after its formation incredibly inspiring as well. When young Franny Pope lost her fight to cancer, her mother, Irish folk singer

Mary O'Dowd and her father, Tony Pope, channeled their grief by raising money for other families facing the same plight. They understood firsthand the emotional stress and overwhelming expense that goes along with caring for a seriously ill child, and they wanted to do something to help other families get through the same challenges. It began with Mary performing local concerts and grew from there. In a small corner of New York City called Yorkville, friends, family, musicians, restaurateurs, clergy, numerous members of the local Electrical Workers Union, as well as members of New York's police and fire departments gathered to support their efforts. Today, many families and young children have been greatly aided because of their efforts. I was incredibly humbled to accept the organization's inaugural Heritage of Hope Award this past spring. I know my mother would have been very proud.

There are countless other examples of people advocating for worthy causes, all too numerous for me to mention here. Perhaps you support the Foundation for AIDS Research, Doctors Without Borders, the Breast Cancer Research Foundation, Action Against Hunger, St. Jude's Children's Research Hospital, or another organization closer to your heart.

Every time I think about how individuals, celebrities, corporations, and governments around the world have responded to crises and have mobilized to provide relief for people in need because of disease, famine, and natural disaster among other hardships, I'm reminded of what a universal impulse advocating and offering help can be. I think it's inherent in the human spirit. We just have to tap into it. It is very powerful to see the kind of change that can happen when people join forces for the larger good like this.

Of course, not every act of advocacy has to occur on such a grand scale. There are many examples of people who need support from us in our daily lives. Increased awareness and communication can help us know who those people are and how we can best help them. One-on-one encouragement and assistance can be gratifying in a very different and very personal way. For instance, it may have been my job to prosecute the assailant who stabbed Star Smith within an inch of her life (you will recall that she is the young woman I mentioned earlier in chapter 2), but it was ultimately my honor to see this almost broken woman reclaim her dignity. The care my team at the LA district attorney's office and I showed her may have helped renew her spirits and get her life back on track, but I cannot tell you what an impact her courage ended up having on me. I admired the way she embraced our help and matched it with her own drive and determination to seek justice and a new start for herself and her child. Her poverty, in stark contrast to all the opportunities I enjoyed in my life, reminded me of just how important it is for me to continue to use the gifts I'd been given for higher purpose.

We will all have a moment in life when a helping hand is needed. Whether the need is great or small, it is important to remember this before that time ever arrives.

As you become better and better at advocating for yourself, please take time out to help people seeking your knowledge, experience, advice, comfort, or nurturing in some way. Meet and talk with them. Find out what they most need to get through their challenge. Think about how your assistance can be offered in such a way as to help them discover their own strength and resiliency.

I remember my father always making time to talk to people who had a budding interest in the work he did. He'd answer all their questions—however long it took. But the thing that impressed me most is that he would also turn the conversation around and ask lots of questions of them. He believed you learn from *everyone*—the hungering mind as well as the knowledgeable mind. In the end, the simple act of listening to what people have to say lets them know that they have knowledge to share too.

If you feel you've learned anything from this book, I ask that you put those lessons to good use for others in addition to yourself. Please make time to advocate for those who don't know how to or who simply can't. Don't just defend them; teach them what you've learned so they know how to advocate for themselves and so they might teach someone else in need too. Help make them stewards of their own fate and a friend to the next person in need.

Both of my parents believed in *paying blessings forward*, and I hope that this book, and all the advice contained in it, is evidence of my belief in that philosophy as well. Of all the lessons they taught me, I am most grateful for this one. I really do want each and every person to know how to represent themselves as well as they possibly can, and to get what they want and need through planning, careful and thoughtful preparation, hard work, clear and effective communication, and perseverance. The more you practice these things, the more they will become second nature to you. The more you advocate for yourself *and* others, the sooner you will become a full-fledged expert in making the case.

I wish you every success in life . . . and in the pursuit of paying that success forward.

ACKNOWLEDGMENTS

My heartfelt thanks goes out to my brother, Anthony Guilfoyle, my dear friends Shawn McSweeney, Susan Shin, Gigi Stone Woods, Eric Bolling, and Dr. Kathryn Smerling, who read and offered wise counsel on the manuscript as it was being written. I'm grateful too for the encouragement of my cohosts on *The Five* and *Outnumbered*, several of whom have been through the publishing process before me with much success. I wish to also thank Roger Ailes, chairman and CEO of Fox News; Bill Shine, senior executive vice president of programming; Suzanne Scott, senior vice president of programming and development at Fox News Channel; Dianne Brandi, executive vice president, legal and business affairs; and John Finley, vice president of development, for fostering an environment that promotes the sharing of ideas and thoughts in all formats. Many thanks as well to Porter Berry, executive producer of *The Five* and *Hannity*; Tommy Firth, senior editorial producer; Sean O'Rourke, associate producer of *The Five* and my segment producer; and the rest of our superstar *Five* production team, Susan, Mina, Amanda, Stefanie, and Allie!

I'm especially grateful for the support and patience of my son, Ronan, who knows that as much fun and hard work as writing this book was he is my greatest joy and worthy of my greatest attentions. Special thanks to the Villency family—Eric, Bob, Rowann, Cara, and Josh—for rallying behind me in this effort and all the rest. (It takes a village to raise a child!) And to the one who champions me in all my pursuits . . . te adoro.

Many thanks also to my literary agent, Mel Berger at WME; my talent agent, Jim Ornstein, also at WME; my friend and at- torney, Marianne Bertuna; and my accountant, Jay Schulman. Lastly, thunderous applause for Lisa Sharkey, senior vice presi- dent and director of creative development, HarperCollins Pub- lishers, for believing in me, acquiring this book, and shepherding it along; for Adam Bellow, editorial director of Broadside Books, an imprint of HarperCollins, for all of his guidance; and for pub- lishing veteran Hope Innelli for her valuable input. Publishing a book is a labor of love that involves many, many people, some of whom are behind-the-scenes advocates who deserve special thanks as well. And as always, a warm-thank you to my fans who are always striving to do, learn, and be more. So glad you picked up this book!

ABOUT THE AUTHOR

KIMBERLY GUILFOYLE is a host of *The Five* and *Outnumbered* on Fox News. She also appears as a legal analyst on *The O'Reilly Factor* and *Hannity*. Before joining Fox in 2006, she was a host of *Both Sides* on Court TV and provided legal analysis for *Anderson Cooper 360*, *Larry King Live*, and ABC's *Good Morning America*. She is a former prosecutor and assistant district attorney, and served as first lady for the City of San Francisco. She was also a deputy district attorney for the Los Angeles County district attorney's office. She currently lives in New York City.